LIGHT IN THE DARK:

THE SEARCH FOR VISIONS

ReVision Publishing

Sebastopol, California

Light in the Dark:

The Search for Visions

by Ruth-Inge Heinze

Edited by Lucy Lewis
Illustrated by Ilse E. Gilliland

Library of Congress Cataloging-in-Publication Data
Heinze, Ruth-Inge, 1919-2007

Light in the Dark: Shamanism, Visions, and Mystical
Experiences / Ruth-Inge Heinze

Includes Index
p. cm.
Includes bibliographical references

ISBN 978-0-9819706-7-7

1. Religion – mysticism
2. Religion – mystical experiences
3. Religion – visions
4. Religion – shamanism
5. Psychology – mind and body
6. Psychology – transpersonal psychology

Cover by Chris Boyd, www.overmanarts.org

Book design by Paula Kline using Adobe® InDesign.®
The typeface used is Franklin Gothic Book for Titles page and
Adobe® Caslon Pro for body text.

Contents

Acknowledgments

I wish to thank the Grandmother Winifred Foundation that encourages the creativity of women over fifty–four to develop and implement projects that enrich one or more aspects of the cultural, educational, social and spiritual well–being of women. I am grateful for their grant which supported my travel and part of the production costs. I am especially indebted to Elizabeth Zinck Rothenberger for encouraging me to finish this book.

I want to thank my parents for giving me life. I want to acknowledge my two high school teachers who evoked in me the love for mathematics and history. I want to thank Josef von Fielitz for putting me on the stage of the Grosse Schauspielhaus in Berlin where I "died" and was reborn as an actress. I am indebted to Professor Murray Emeneau for introducing me to the beauty of Sanskrit and Pali. I did not always agree with Alan Dundes, Professor of Folklore at the University of California, Berkeley, but he certainly inspired me to look for meaning in the daily manifestations of life.

I want to thank Max Zeller for calling the Bruno Klopfer seminars at Asilomar and Hawaii so that Jungian analysts could discuss their latest findings and intensify their dreams. I want to thank my meditation teacher in Chaing Mai, Thailand, and the Ven. U. Silananda at the Burmese monastery in Daly City, California, for laying a sound basis for my meditation. I want to thank Stephen Chang for teaching me internal exercises and the science of Chinese herbs. And I want to thank the Singapore clinic for allowing me to practice acupuncture.

I want to thank the mediums and shamans in Southeast Asia for inviting me into their houses and sharing their knowledge with me.

I want to thank all workshop participants in the United States, Russia, Lithuania, and Estonia for allowing me to use excerpts from their stories in this book.

I want to thank Ilse E. Gilliland for her delightful and intuitive drawings.

I want to thank my friends in the United States, Europe (Germany, France, England, Hungary, Italy, Lithuania, Estonia, Romania, Russia), Asia (India, Nepal, Sri Lanka, Burma, Thailand, Malaysia, Singapore, Indonesia, the Philippines, Hong Kong, China, Taiwan, Japan, Korea), Australia and New Zealand for their support in the "dance."

I want to thank the universe for sustaining me while I was clearing my "glass" so that the Divine could shine through.

Ruth-Inge Heinze
Berkeley, December 1994

RUTH-INGE HEINZE:
INCARNATING THE VISION
Foreword by Stanley Krippner

It was a pleasure to read this memoir by my dear friend Ruth- Inge Heinze. It includes an ethnoautobiography in which she traces her father's roots back to both the persecuted French Huguenots who escaped to West Prussia and to generations of German artisans in the area surrounding Berlin. Her mother's family also hailed from West Prussia and Ruth- Inge spent many summers helping relatives at harvest time. Once she was entrusted with caring for the sheep and was shocked to see the animals frolicking with abandon. When told that they had ingested clover, she was introduced to the world of mind- altering plants, which she was to rediscover in her studies of shamanism decades later.

Ruth- Inge was a transformative force in the lives of many people, and it was remarkable to read of her own transformations over time. In this book, she describes her parents as conscientious but unemotional, a trait surprising to those who know of her passionate opinions. Nonetheless, her mother was known for her generosity and her father cultivated a garden that saved the family from starvation during the bleak years of the Second World War and its aftermath. As a young child, Ruth- Inge was standing along on a Baltic Sea beach when she experienced a sense of oneness with the sun, the winds, and the sea. Following what she calls "this interconnectedness," Ruth- Inge's parents thought he had suffered a heat stroke and kept her in bed for several days.

Throughout this book, Ruth- Inge laments the lack of visions in the contemporary era and spends considerable time defining and describing visions and the role they play in individual and social transformations. She observes how incarnating her visions and dreams kept her alive, giving her the strength to continue her work. Her childhood feeling of "interconnectedness" gave her a standard gauge against which to measure later experiences as to whether or not they were genuine. She was again transformed after making her debut as a stage actress and, once more, when she arrived in the United States in 1955 where she found work as a translator and editor. Living on a shoestring, she found ways to visit the Blackfoot Indians of Wyoming and began to collect their mythological stories. She explored Mayan pyramids, toured many Asian countries, and paid her respect to the graves of Sufi poets in Iran. Back in the United States, she founded a German-American theater group and initiated a "universal dialogue" seminar in her apartment. After a stint in the Peace Corps, Ruth-Inge returned to Berlin to care for her ailing parents and, while there, began to study anthropology at the city's Free University. After her parents' death, she returned to the United States and, at the age of 48, became an undergraduate at the University of California in Berkeley.

Ruth-Inge received her Ph.D. in Asian Studies in 1974 and soon received a research grant to continue the research in India and Southeast Asia that had served as the topic for her doctorate. This continual reinvention of herself had taken Ruth-Inge into "darkness," but her novel remedy was to enlist a drummer to produce a percussive rhythm while she sat silently. Her ensuing vision of "Infinite Light" provided a glimpse of what she felt shamans and mystics experience. Hence, in 1978 she was awarded a Fulbright-Hays Research Grant to study shamans and mediums in Southeast Asia, and returned from time to time for the rest of her life. Despite these many accomplishments, she only received an appointment as a "Lecturer" at the University of California, Berkeley: I was appalled by the cramped quarters of her office during my first visit to see her there. We had met earlier at my office at Saybrook University in San Francisco, where I was able to secure a position for her as a "Distinguished Consulting Faculty Member." She had been well treated at Mills College in Oakland, her first academic appointment after receiving her doctorate. However, her course on the religious traditions of India had to be discontinued because it lacked students; the slot was given to a more popular business course on accounting.

Ruth-Inge had both the insight and energy to launch organizations and conferences, notably the annual International Conference on the Study of Shamanism and Alternative Modes of Healing. Since the first meeting in 1984, this meeting has brought together scholars, practitioners, and laypeople at a cozy retreat center at Dominican University in San Rafael, California. The official sponsor was the Independent Scholars of Asia, another group founded by Ruth-Inge. These meetings have featured indigenous shamans from such diverse countries as Brazil, Cambodia, Ecuador, Mongolia, and Zimbabwe. The Mongolian shamans returned several times, once giving Ruth-Inge an award in recognition for her work in preserving shamanic traditions. But their first visit was far from facile. Having received a governmental travel grant, they asked a travel agency to book them a flight for California and ended up in Los Angeles. After an all-night (and expensive) taxi ride to Dominican University, they arrived in time for their presentation filled with enthusiasm and energy.

In 1992, Ruth-Inge and I were members of a group of scholars who attended a humanistic psychology conference in Moscow. She conducted a well-received workshop on shamanic journeying, providing her own drum and instructions synthesized from those she had learned from her decades-long interactions with shamans. After the conference, a few of us conducted workshops in Novosibirsk, Siberia. Because Siberian practitioners played a historic role in the anthropological construction of the term "shaman," one might think that Ruth-Inge was bringing the proverbial "coals to Newcastle." On the contrary. Shamanism was driven underground by zealous Marxists following their overthrow of the Czar. Shamans were murdered, just as they had been killed by zealous Christians following the European invasion of the Americas in the 1500s. Ruth-Inge and I interviewed a local folk healer who attended our workshops in an attempt to learn what she could incorporate into her own practice. During our final celebration, we all sang Beatles' songs that had been laboriously typed up with multiple carbon copies. Upon my return to the United States, I sent our hosts a copy of the complete Beatles songbook, much to their delight.

Ruth-Inge's small Berkeley apartment served as the venue for a monthly dream seminar during the last years of her life. The numbers of participants varied from month to month, but it never exceeded the available space. Ruth-Inge was a gracious host, providing her own delicious blend of herbal tea to accompany the snacks brought by participants. The dream group used a person-centered method of dreamwork pioneered by Montague Ullman, a New York psychoanalyst with whom I had worked for many years. After a participant related his or her dream, the other members of the group reacted by saying, "If this were my dream…," and give an interpretation that might or might not evoke resonance with the dreamer.

Ruth-Inge's comments were always perceptive and filled with insight.

A long-time meditator, Ruth-Inge was not always calm and serene. Once, when her annual shamanism conference was interrupted by a surprise birthday celebration, she was gratified but also a bit indignant as she tried desperately to restore the lost time so that speakers would not be penalized by the festivities. On another occasion, a member of our study group visiting Prague said that we should rethink our hectic schedule to give Ruth-Inge a chance to relax. She retorted, "I will relax when I am dead. Right now there is too much to see and do to think of dropping anything from our list." When a speaker went overtime at one of our shamanism conference, Ruth-Inge was prone to stand up and announce the next speaker. On such occasions, she did not suffer fools gladly.

Ruth-Inge's transformation from a wartime survivor to a dramatic actress to a world traveler to a student (and practitioner) of shamanism is a remarkable story of survival and evolution. Highly respected among cultural anthropologists and that small multidisciplinary group of scholars who recognize the value of shamanic traditions, she-by her own admittance-lived at least seven lifetimes. The books that she wrote or edited are a continual resource for men and women eager to revisit the ancient wisdom to be found in shamanism, Eastern philosophy, and sacred texts and mythic stories. She guided doctoral research at Saybrook University and elsewhere, spawning new generations of researchers who have renounced the mid-20th century depiction of shamans as neurotics at best and psychotics at worst. Her incredible book is a treasure chest of anecdotes, case studies, exercises, and theoretical material that displays Ruth-Inge's incredible erudition, most of it gained not only from library tomes but from personal interactions in village huts, esoteric temples, humid rain forests, festive celebrations, and silent ashrams. Did she leave a memorable legacy? Undoubtedly so. Will there be another like her? Probably not.

Stanley Krippner, Ph.D.

SPECIAL THANKS

To Lucy Lewis, Ruth-Inge's dear friend and colleague, for her loving devotion in editing this text. It was a joy to work with Lucy as she perused each word so that the author's voice would be distinctly heard throughout the manuscript. It has been an honor and privilege to hear Lucy's stories of her travels and rich experiences with Ruth-Inge.

To Jürgen Kremer for his determination to get *Light in the Dark* published. This book would not be here if not for his persistence, expertise and thoughtful suggestions. He worked tirelessly to prepare the illustrations for digital publication.

To Elizabeth Zinck Rothenberger for helping to see the manuscript to fruition.

To Kathleen Taugher for helping with Ruth-Inge's photographs. Her enthusiasm for this book is inspiring and invaluable.

To Chris Boyd for his ongoing support for ReVision Publishing and the creation of the beautiful cover.

To Paula Kine for layout and design and help with editing.

We would like to extend our appreciation and gratitude to William Ronald for contributing his editorial skills during the first round of proofing the manuscript.

To Diana Vandenberg for capturing the essence of Ruth in paint. We were unable to contact the estate of Ms. Vandenberg to ascertain permission for the use of the painting as book cover. Copyright holders are asked to contact the publisher at www.revisionpublishing.org.

Ruth-Inge Heinze Timeline

November 4, 1919: Born in Berlin, Germany. Only child of Otto and Luise Heinze. On her father's side, 1/8 French Huguenot. One of her French ancestors co–founded the Charite, a large hospital where famous physicians have worked over the years. The other roots on her father's side are in the mark Brandenburg province surrounding Berlin. Some were skippers, most were artisans. Her mother was born in West Prussia, in a small village close to the (former) Polish border. Her relatives in West Prussia were farmers. She was proud to discover that her maternal grandfather had been a healer.

1937: Completed course at a commercial college, and began work as secretary for the rector of the University of Berlin.

1937–1938: Worked in the country in Arbeitsdienst (Labor Service).

1938: Since she spoke several languages, she was hired to assist foreign visitors.

1939–1943: Studied acting in Berlin, Dresden and Vienna.

1945–1948: Worked as actress in Mecklenburg, Nestreliz, Guben and other towns in East Germany.

1949–1955: Convened a writer's group (Group of the Twelve).

1955: Came to America. Began work as an editor for Wilcox & Follett, in Chicago; she also reviewed manuscripts in the children's book division. She took courses at the University of Chicago.

1956–1962: Moved to San Francisco, and worked as a technical translator for an international engineering company. She founded a German–American theater group–the Art Repertory Theater. They played comedies and tragedies at San Francisco and Santa Clara State Universities, Monterey Language Institute, University of California, Berkeley and the City Club in San Francisco. She also held twice monthly meetings for literary readings. This was the start of the Universal Dialogue.

1962: Became an American citizen. Volunteered for the Peace Corps and trained for work in Thailand.

1963: Returned to Germany to care for dying parents. Also taught adult education course in Anthropology, English and French. Passed the great Latinum, and studied Anthropology, Sanskrit, and Southeast Asian cultures at the Free University of Berlin.

1968–1974: Studied anthropology at U.C. Berkeley. Was awarded a B.A. in 1969, with a thesis on the social–cultural comparison of a Thai custom. Ph.D. in Asian studies awarded in 1974, with a dissertation on the role of Buddhism in Thailand.

1971-2: Conducted field work in Thailand

1974: Taught Indian Religions at Mills College in Oakland. Founded Independent Scholars of Asia which teaches other scholars how to continue their professional work without the backing of a university.

1975: Received a post–doctoral grant to India.

1978: Awarded a Fulbright– Hays Research Grant to study shamans and mediums in Southeast Asia. For a year, was stationed at the Institute of Southeast Asia Studies in Singapore, and traveled repeatedly to Thailand, Malaysia, Indonesia, the Philippines, Sumatra, Sabah and Saraka.

1983–1990: Lectured on cruises to Asia.

1984-2007 Organizes annual shamanism conference at Santa Sabina Center in San Rafael, CA. See www.shamanismconference.org for further information.

1992 Workshop presentation at the Conference for Humanistic Psychology in Moscow.

1995 Appointed Distinguished Consulting Faculty Member at Saybrook University, San Francisco. [I am checking with Stanley Krippner on this date, I will let you know whether it's correct]

2007, July 20 Ruth-Inge Heinze passes on.

1. Overview

Introduction

*It is important that awake people be awake,
or a breaking line may discourage them back to sleep;
the signals we give—yes or no, or maybe—
should be clear: the darkness around us is deep.*

William Stafford (1993:15)

I wrote this book because our world lacks visions. Most of us forgot what visions are. And what is worse, we no longer explore our full potential.

I will, therefore, discuss the phenomenon of vision and then tell my story before I offer some suggestions how we can open ourselves to the "Source."

If we have lost the connection, we can reconnect. But we cling to the past instead of staying in the present. We should know that we are constantly moving from "Here to Here." The magic formula is "staying in the moment."

The Buddha had already talked about "direct consciousness" two and a half thousand years ago. We are the guardians of our own strength, but we don't cultivate our inner potential. "Energy management" is discussed publicly now because natural resources are dwindling, and species and landscapes are disappearing, right in front of our eyes. We are so involved in satisfying material needs that there seems to be no time left to look beyond issues of plain survival. And, on top of it, we lost the faculty of putting the pieces of the puzzle together.

Historians of religion tell us that Cosmic Energy belongs to the Realm Without Form where worldly conditions have been transcended. This leads us to believe that, as long as we live in the Realm of Consensus (which is also the Realm of Desire), the access to that mystical Source will stay obscured. But, as soon as we learn to transcend the ever changing "reality of the moment," the limitations of time and space disappear, and we can access the Source at anytime and anywhere in the Here and Now.

When everything—our past, present, and future—can be found in the Infinite Source, why don't we tap this inexhaustible treasure? Why do we hold on to our confusion and feel trapped in the jaws of helplessness? Why don't we look for the connection which restores what has gotten out of balance? Why do we obstruct the process of realization?

The Infinite Source has been called "Akashic Records" by Hindus; we talk of Intuitive Knowledge, God, Infinite Wisdom, or Cosmic Energy. When energy remains static, inertia sets in and the energy becomes self-destructive. Energy has to move.

Myths around the world speak, indeed, of the Eternal Renewal, the Infinite Cycle of Creation. This dynamic cycle is necessary to regenerate. Maintaining the momentum is also essential for protecting the purity of the Source.

The only constant in our life is, indeed, our connection with the Infinitely Moving Divine Energy. When we are in the middle of the stream, the banks of the river seem to flow by. We are no longer attached to anything impermanent. Nourished by the Source, we can "dance in the middle of the stream" and be a conscious part of the Infinite Cycle of Creation. Look at the snake that sheds its skin every year! Look at the phoenix who rises from the fire!

Ironically, what we fear most is change. We know our fears and anxieties, but we forgot how to renew ourselves. We are caught in the cave into which civilization has led us and judge reality from the shadows cast against the walls of the cave. Having lost our capacity to rise from ignorance and darkness, we no longer recognize the simplest manifestation of the Source. And when we become aware of such manifestations, we discard them.

We are still consumed by the fire, but we hold on to the ashes whose only redeeming purpose is to fertilize the ground. Has the gap between "vision" and "consensus reality" widened so much that visions appear to be "wishful thinking"? Why do we no longer dare to hope? Why have we buried our faculty to have visions? Why do we ignore the Infinite Source which can be found deep inside of us? Rainer Maria Rilke said,

> We have already had to rethink so many of our concepts of motion, we will also gradually learn to realize that that which we call destiny goes forth from within people, not from without into them. Only because so many have not absorbed their destinies and transmuted them within themselves while they were living in them, have they not recognized what has gone forth out of them; it was so strange to them that, in their bewildered fright, they thought it must only just then have entered into them, for they swear never before to have found anything like it in themselves. As people were long mistaken about the motion of the sun, so they are even yet mistaken about the motion of that which is to come. The future stands firm...but we move in infinite space (1992:48).

We are caught between two worlds, the finite and the infinite. Having forgotten that we move in infinite space, we have lost sight of the bridge over which visions come to us.

However, there are visionaries in the twentieth century. They have the same problem as most of their predecessors. They remain misunderstood because the Mind/Matter controversy has not yet been resolved. We have, therefore, to be aware of the deficiencies in our understanding of reality. We have to develop views which take other dimensions into consideration.

The first sound we hear is the heart beat of our mother. This rhythmic beat entrains us already in the womb and conveys love, protection, and the feeling of being embedded in a living organism. After we have been born into this world, most of us forget that we continue to be embedded in a living organism. Why don't we listen to the heart beat of the universe?

❧ ❧ ❧

Our first question should be, "How and when do visions arise?" For over sixty years, I have been asking colleagues, students, relatives, friends and acquaintances in the United States, Europe, Asia, Australia, and New Zealand this question. I found that some visions appeared "unsolicited." Those reporting "spontaneous" events were, as Michael Murphy confirmed, men and women, young and old, in widely disparate situations, [who] at times experience the unitive awareness, selfless love, and redeeming joy that crown human life. I have come to believe that virtually every one of us has experienced these spontaneous feelings; and that everyone of us can cultivate moments when the ordinary becomes extraordinary, when mind and body are graced by something beyond themselves (1992:6).

Visions appear after fasting. They arise after long and ardent prayer and many years of spiritual exercises. Visions emerge on their own at times of great tranquility when our mind is ready to open up to new possibilities. Visions appear also at times of conflict and despair because our mind cannot go any other way.

* * *

Why do visionaries have problems talking about their experience? Many psychiatrists, as well as psychologists, still consider "having visions" to be an abnormal faculty. But, most of all, everybody who desperately is looking for answers to existential questions, strongly resents anybody who claims to have found the "light." Expecting to be "shown the light," many of us do not want to invest any effort to find the light on our own. However, "right effort" is an important link of the Eightfold Way in Buddhism, it is essential for any spiritual path. Watch out for those who attach negative connotations to the word "discipline." Only "disciplined commitment" can lead to en-lighten-ment.

When we want to invite our contemporaries to trust their "inner voice," we have to raise their curiosity so that they develop a yearning and want to discover the full range of their own faculties.

* * *

The world has been given to us. Daily we are experiencing the miracle of creation. Daily the sun rises without fail. Daily the earth turns around the sun. All those who lived through wars and catastrophes naturally greet the Light of the Day each morning. Why do we need tragic events to wake us up so that we begin to honor again the Eternal Dynamic Energy daily with the rising sun? How many of us show, each day, their appreciation of this eternal cycle? How many of us enjoy "movement"?

The Divine Source can be felt when we stand at the ocean and become one with the ever moving sun, the wind and the waves. We can become energized by leaning against a tree, feeling its life energy flowing through us. We can become grounded, sitting on a rock, and then suddenly feel its changes, because even a rock is touched by the mystical "Turner of the Wheel." We can become energized, lying in a meadow, growing with the flowers and the grass. We can be moved and we can move ourselves!

We have to recognize where and when we have stopped resonating. We were not always insensitive. Who and what has stunted our perceptions? There is no excuse for turning our backs on what is sustaining us. We have to move away from the feeling that we are trapped in darkness.

Yes, we have to face chaos and ignorance, and, most of all, we have to defend the Source against pollution.

The light is in us and we have to carry this light into the darkness. We have to make a conscious effort to carry the all-encompassing light into the darker aspects of this existence. We can interconnect! Everybody can experience wholeness!

To accept the concept of wholeness as an intellectual construct is fairly easy, but many of us feel uncomfortable in applying the principle of cosmic interconnectedness to physical laws.

First, we have to recognize that we experience on at least five levels — the physical, the emotional, the mental, the social, and the spiritual. On whatever level an event is first recognized, the experience is inextricably tied to each of the other levels and involves all levels. So all these "impressions" become part of our memory bank. A social disadvantage may cause unhappy feelings and this mental stress can manifest on the physical level. Spiritual yearning can go both ways. It can either muster the forces and all levels begin to work toward the goal, or it depresses action on all levels and so reinforces the inertia by feeding into feelings of defeat. These are only two of numerous other examples with different combinations.

We have to learn how to excavate our knowledge on all levels so that we can more easily access our visionary potential. What greater discovery can there be than to realize that the advice and support we need can be found inside of us.

※ ※ ※

A *caveat*, however, is in place. We have to look at our visions carefully not to mistake "wishful thinking" for a vision. On the other hand, we may discard some of our best visions because we suspect they may be hallucinations. Murphy warned that, "All of our capacities, whether normal or metanormal, somatic or extrasomatic, are subject to the limitations and distortions produced by our inherited and socially-conditioned nature" (1992:92).

He continued, citing Myers,

> Hidden in the deep of our being is a rubbish heap, as well as, a treasure-house; degenerations and insanities, as well as, beginnings of higher development. The intermingling of metanormal with abnormal elements, of psychic rubbish with psychic treasure, occurs in religious and philosophic, as well as, artistic works. Indeed, inspiration in any field can be clouded by various pathologies. To experience it over time without distortion, to develop a lasting capacity for it, most of us need disciplined commitment to creative work, as well as, developing self-knowledge (1992:136).

As a measuring rod for the authenticity of visions, I personally accept only those visions which are clear and "feel right" in every aspect. When there is any doubt, I go with the doubt. We can always ask our inner voice "to come again." Nothing ever gets lost. If the message is important, it will keep knocking at our door.

⊕ ⊕ ⊕

This book has been written to talk about visions in our time. We can access, decode, and be empowered by them.

We need visions to write the mythology of our times and we have to create rituals which convey meaning through action. Many voices are emerging from the dark. We can join them.

There is not only hope, there is certitude and infinite wisdom!

We can no longer build our future on fears and anxieties. We need to discover our latent faculties so that we can rise from the darkness which seems to close in on us.

Listening to our visions, we can muster the courage to confront darkness wherever it appears. Darkness is ignorance. We *know* that we have to carry the Light into the Darkness.

Listening to the Inner Source, we learn to uncover the Inner Light. New insights trigger shifts in our consciousness and we begin to experience surges of energy. We re-cognize the road signs which indicate the directions our efforts should take. We can become catalysts, first to ourselves and then to others.

We need visions to live by.

What Are Visions?

...within man is the soul of the whole;
the wise silence; the universal beauty,
to which every part and particle is equally related;
the eternal One.
And this deep power in which we exist
and whose beatitude is all accessible to us,
is not only self-sufficing and perfect in every hour,
but the act of seeing and the thing seen,
the seer and the spectacle,
the subject and the object are one.

...the soul in man is not an organ
...is not a function...is not a faculty,
but a light;
is not the intellect or the will,
but the master of the intellect and the will;
is the background of our being.
...a light shines through us upon all things
...the light is all.

Ralph Waldo Emerson, 1884:219

The word "vision" was used in the thirteenth century by Thomas Aquinas when he recognized "supernatural manifestations." In our century, six hundred years later, "visions" are interpreted in many different ways. In Mircea Eliade's *Encyclopedia of Religions*, a "vision" is identified as being

> a religious experience that involves seeing and, frequently, other senses as well. The quality of the experience suggests that the content of the perception is real, a direct, unmediated contact with a non-ordinary aspect of reality that is external and independent of the perceiver (quoted from Goodman, 1987:282).

Mystics and poets have reported that this "contact with a non-ordinary aspect of reality" occurs deep inside of us. In *Webster's Ninth New Collegiate Dictionary*, "vision" is

1a. something seen in a dream, trance, or ecstasy; esp., a supernatural appearance that conveys a revelation;
1b. an object of imagination;
1c. a manifestation to the senses of something immaterial;

2a. the act or power of imagination;
2bi. mode of seeing or conceiving;
bii. unusual discernment or foresight;

2c. direct mystical awareness of the supernatural, usually in visible form;
3a. the act or power of seeing;
3b. the special sense by which the qualities of an object (color, luminosity, shape and size) constituting its appearance are perceived and which is mediated by the eye

To repeat: When "supernatural appearances" convey "revelations," we can speak of "direct mystical awareness of the supernatural." But why do we call it supernatural? What is supernatural? Isn't everything part of the Whole? Haven't we closed the doors to the main source of information? As I said before, we live in Plato's cave which civilization has built for us, and we judge life by looking at the shadows on the cave walls.

Furthermore, all those who have experienced visions did receive information which changed their lives; but they hesitate to talk about these experiences because visions (or any mystical events, for that matter) do not fit into the scientific model of the 20th century.

Searching for official opinions about visions, I found a Congressional Record which included proceedings and debates of the 93rd Congress of the United States of America, First Session, Vol. 119:141, Washington, Tuesday, September 25, 1973, during which an article of Dr. Stanley R. Dean, M.D., Miami, on "Metapsychiatry: The Interface between Psychiatry and Mysticism" was presented. Dean talked about metapsychiatry as "a semantically congruent term...to designate the important but hitherto unclassified interface between psychiatry and mysticism" and said

> psychic research is a legitimate concern of psychiatry, the specialty best qualified to investigate phenomena, assess validity and expose fallacy in matters of the mind. There can be little doubt that reciprocal enlightenment would result if Psychiatry lent its expertise to the religious and philosophic speculations that have hitherto preempted that field (1973).

He quoted the former president of the American Medico-Psychological Association, Dr. Richard Maurice Bucke, a distinguished pioneer in the field. Bucke had presented a paper entitled "Cosmic Consciousness" at the annual meeting in Philadelphia, in May 1894. Four years later he published a book under the same title in which he developed the theory that

> a seemingly miraculous higher consciousness, appearing sporadically throughout the ages, was a *natural* [emphasis mine] rather than an occult phenomenon, that it was latent in all of us, and was, in fact, an evolutionary process that would eventually raise all mankind to a higher level of existence.

> Cosmic consciousness refers to a supra-sensory, supra-rational level of mentation that transcends all other human experience and creates a sense of Oneness with the universe. Its existence has been

known since antiquity under a variety of regional and ritual terms — Nirvana, Samadhi, Kairos, Unio Mystica, to name but a few.

...large scale government-sponsored research in Soviet countries...resulted in some startling psychic discoveries....The United States Army's Intelligence Agency has for some time recognized the power of mental telepathy, and warns about it in a manual published by the Technical Bulletin Department of the Provost Marshall General's Office, entitled, "Techniques of Surveillance and Undercover Investigation" (op.cit.)

Having surveyed ancient and modern literature and liturgies, Dean stated that the ultraconscious manifests in the following ways:

1. The onset is ushered in by an awareness of light that floods the brain and fills the mind....
2. The individual is bathed in emotions of supercharged joy, rapture, triumph, grandeur, reverential awe and wonder....
3. A noetic illumination occurs that is quite impossible to describe. In an intuitive flash one has an awareness of the meaning and drift of the universe, an identification and merging with Creation, infinity and immortality, a depth beyond depth of revealed meaning — in short, a conception of an Over-Self, so omnipotent that religion has interpreted it as God.
4. There is a feeling of transcendental love and compassion for all living things.

5. Fear of death falls off like a mantle; physical and mental suffering vanish....

6. There is a reappraisal of the material things in light, an enhanced appreciation of beauty.

7. There is an extraordinary quickening of the intellect, an uncovering of latent genius and leadership.

8. There is a sense of mission. The revelation is so moving and profound that the individual is moved to share it with all fellow men.

9. A charismatic change occurs in personality—an inner and outer radiance, as though charged with some divinely inspired power, a magnetic force that attracts and inspires others.

10. There is a sudden or gradual development of extraordinary psychic gifts such as clairvoyance, extrasensory perception, telepathy, precognition, healing, etc. Though generally regarded as occult, such phenomena may have a more rational explanation. They may be due to an awakening of transhuman powers of perception latent in all of us (op.cit.).

I share Dean's opinion that this "ultraconsciousness" is

> a genuine metamorphosis of consciousness that has been experienced by certain sages, prophets and leaders, men of genius through the ages. The factors producing it are as yet unknown, but the remarkable uniformity of distinguishing characteristics, regardless of origin, should leave no doubt that a common denominator—empirically validated if not yet scientifically proven—underlies all of them (op.cit.).

Dean also cited Jan Ehrenwald, Jule Eisenbud, Berthold Schwarz, Ian Stevenson, Montague Ullman and others. This 1994 report is one of the first official acknowledgments of other dimensions in our century.

Who really knows what visions are? Visions are experiences of spiritual reality, acceptable to the fields of theology, comparative religion, philosophy, and recently, transpersonal psychology. Shouldn't we, therefore, turn to these disciplines and ask them to teach us the forgotten ways to the Source?

Eastern religions offer some clues. Hinduism and Buddhism clearly define the levels of consciousness on the way to the Highest Goal of Transcendence, the Unio Mystica. Approximately two thousand years ago, in India, Patanjali, e.g., collected 196 yoga sutras which tell us *How to Know God* (Prabhavananda, 1953). Practice of yoga and other forms of meditation prepare for the journey and meditation manuals spell out the different states on the way to en-lighten-ment. Eastern philosophies and psychologies are now taught in the United States. Why haven't we availed ourselves of these possibilities? It becomes clear that no goal, whether spiritual or not, can be reached without effort and without the "disciplined commitment" Murphy (1992:136) is talking about. Why do we shy away from "discipline" and "commitment"?

But there are other traditions which also openly talk about visions. In Judeo-Christian literature, e.g., the Bible, we find numerous accounts about visionary experiences of prophets (Moses, the apocalyptic visions of St. John, etc.). There are legends about saints, e.g., Santa Teresa, and, more explicitly, the spiritual exercises of St. Ignatius of Loyola (Mottola, 1990). Ample data are also available on practices and revelations of

Muslims (Schi'ites, as well as, Sufis) and Taoist revelations on sacred mountains, e.g., Mao Shan.

For millennia, shamans have gone on "vision quests." These predecessors of codified religions are still effective in modern societies. We can find shamans who work easily outside or inside the framework of world religions. Lame Deer, for example, said in 1970,

> Crying for a vision, that's the beginning of all religion. The thirst for a dream from above, without this you are nothing. This I believe. It is like the prophets in your bible, like Jesus fasting in the desert, getting his visions. It's like our Sioux vision quest, the *hanblecheya*. White men have forgotten this. God no longer speaks to them from a burning bush. If he did, they wouldn't believe it, and call it science fiction.

> Your old prophets went into the desert crying for a dream and the desert gave it to them. But the white men of today have made a desert of their religion and a desert within themselves. The White Man's desert is a place without dreams or life. Nothing grows there. But the spirit water is always way down there to make the desert green again (Erdoes, 1990:28).

At the International Shaman Conference in 1993, Felicitas Goodman spoke of religious specialists who "take it upon themselves to reconstitute the 'consciousness of the heavens', 'the cosmic order', by means of specific rituals." Goodman talked about such complex spirit journey during which the practitioner, the shamaness, reached the area of the "consciousness of the heavens," a region of "multidimensional patterns" in the Upper World and repaired the torn web. Mythological accounts confirm our experimental findings. For instance, according to a Zuni myth (Cushing, 1986:150-174), a young man who had disturbed the cosmic order by repeatedly neglecting to bring the ritual offering to the deer's spirit after killing it, has to undertake a spirit journey.... He finally arrives at Sun Father to make matters right. In other words, the spirit journey to the Upper World has been recognized as the strategy of choice for a cosmic disorder produced by inappropriate human activity (Goodman, 1993:264).

The spirit journey was for hunters and gatherers a "preferred religious activity" and

is equally well known also to horticulturalists... however, horticulturalists apparently do not engage in spirit journeys as widely as do the hunter-gatherers, and when they do, they seem to be occupied with less weighty matters than reordering the cosmos. As we know from the anthropological literature, they travel mainly to the Lower World for various specific activities, connected with healing. There are local traditions in the American Southwest....that Pueblo Indian medicine men "go flying" over the Middle World, fulfilling what amounts to a social obligation.... In fact, there are indications that some horticulturalists felt their ability of journeying to the Upper World to be slipping away entirely. The German anthropologist Kurt Nimuendaju...who for years lived with Guarani groups on the coast of Brazil at the beginning of the twentieth century, was told that in earlier times humans had the ability to "make their bodies light," and then they were able to visit First Woman's magic corn garden. Now, however, they contended, people were no longer able to do that (Goodman, 1993:264).... Given the fact that humans could no longer accomplish the spirit journey in its most power- ful form, where simply by assuming a particular posture and rhythmically stimulating their body, they would be catapulted out into the cosmic ranges (Goodman, 1993:265).

Goodman then suggested that the Nazca lines in Peru could be superimpositions of the "correct" pattern on the universal web which had been disturbed by incorrect human behavior. Shamans act, indeed, like "telegraph operators" in correcting the defects in the universal pattern caused by humans.

Over five hundred years ago, during the Renais- sance, science and religion split and the connections between mind and body, emotions and soul, were arti- ficially severed.

When all that could be called "religious" (natu- ralistically as well as supernaturalistically) was cut away from science, from knowledge, from fur- ther discovery, from the possibility of skeptical investigation, from the possibility of purifying and improving, such a dichotomized religion was doomed (Maslow, 1971:13).

Without spiritual dimensions, science was doomed also. Memories of the interconnectedness faded and it became more and more difficult to find the bridge. However, we still yearn for the Source and continue to believe in Wholeness.

Some explorers of the realm of matter have finally recognized their own limitations and 20th-century physicists added new dimensions to their paradigms, e.g., Bohm spoke of the explicate and implicate order (1983).

Despite some promising developments, many contemporary scientists still ignore the visionary process. Mistrusting the intrinsic nature and capacity of man, they just don't know what to do with anything outside the realm of matter. Diagnostic manuals for psychiatrists and psychologists like the *DSM-III-R*, for example, ignored large areas of human experience and were not helpful in distinguishing visions from hallucinations, active imagination, and wishful thinking. (As I am writing these lines, I learned that, thanks to courageous colleagues, a new category has been added to the *DSM-IV* which allows diagnosing "religious or spiritual experiences" as not necessarily being pathological).

Without much help from the hard sciences, we can consult reports of visionaries whose experiences have been acknowledged (e.g., by church authorities, in retrospect). We can measure our experiences against these reports. (For detailed information on "Our Roots: The American Visionary Tradition," see Taylor, 1993:6-17).

There are also problems with communication. Visionaries have to translate the ineffable messages into ordinary language. So visionaries, shamans and mystics have used symbols and rituals to convey interconnectedness. Evelyn Underhill confirmed that

> The mystic cannot wholly do without symbol and image, inadequate to his vision though they must always be; for his experience must be expressed if it is to be communicated, and its actuality is inexpressible except in some hint or parallel which will stimulate the dormant intuition of the reader and convey, as all poetic language does, something beyond its surface sense (1955:79).

She used four characteristics for recognizing the mystical state of consciousness,

1. being active and practical which rules out a passive state of contemplation [because she believes that true mystical experiences demand to be acted upon];
2. being concerned with the spiritual and transcendental, not the cosmological;
3. [the mystic is] not inclined toward loving optimism and monism in a philosophical regard for some object of reality, the unity of a mystic experience is "a living and personal Object of Love";
4. the unity is a living relationship which involves "a definite psychological experience," "a definite state or form of enhanced life." It is "a genuine life process and not an intellectual speculation" (1955:81).

Deikman, on the other hand, distinguished between

1. untrained sensate
2. trained sensate, and
3. trained

transcendent experiences (1969:24).

Spontaneous visions reveal themselves to the untrained when "conditions are right." Prolonged contemplative practices lead, sooner or later, to trained sensate experiences (though untrained and trained sensate states are "phenomenologically indistinguishable"). The experiences of trained transcendent practitioners (i.e., mystics), however, conform "more closely to the specific religious cosmology to which they are accustomed."

Mystics have completed the deautomatization process and are usually supported by "a formal social structure." Their visions are repeatable and tend "to have a more significant and persisting psychological effect" (Deikman 1969:25). In other words, only trained transcendent practitioners are mystics; individuals belonging to the first two categories are visionaries.

The five principal features of mystic experiences are for Deikman:

1. intense realness,
2. unusual sensations,
3. unity,
4. ineffability, and
5. trans-sensate phenomena (1969:35).

The five phases of Underhill's mystic path are:

1. awakening, where the Self becomes joyously aware of the existence of the One;
2. acquisition of self-knowledge or purgation where the Self painfully turns away from the content of the senses toward the Absolute; which leads to the happiness of
3. the Self getting a vision-without-union-of the Absolute [which Underhill considers to be the great stage of illumination];
4. the surrender, purification of the spirit, or the Dark Night of the Soul, where the human instinct for human happiness must be killed, to emerge cleansed of the individuality and volition of the Self;
5. to achieve peace through the Union of the Self with the Absolute (1955:169ff).

When we are talking about the "Union," there can no longer be polarities. There can neither be light nor darkness, everything is in the infinite stream of cosmic consciousness. Bucke found that

> in its more striking instances [cosmic consciousness] is not simply an expansion or extension of the self-conscious mind with which we are all familiar, but the super-addition of a function as distinct from any possessed by the average man as self-consciousness is distinct from any function possessed by the higher animals (1961:1-3).

I firmly believe that one of the most important activities for scientific exploration is the inclusion and expansion of empirical processes. We start with acknowledging that we are awake and we observe our mental, emotional, physical, but also spiritual activities. We can train ourselves to take our "awareness" into the experience of spiritual processes. We can develop methods of recognizing and using inner experiences.

Scholarly books tell us that many scientific discoveries came, for example, in dreams. In other words, the incentive for change comes from a deep inner source. We have the capacity to excavate and cultivate the dormant seeds so that they can grow to a point where we are able to realize all connections in the everyday world.

❀ ❀ ❀

There seem to be two ways — the mysticism of introspection and the mysticism of unifying vision (Otto, 1957:ix). Stace also talks about two types of mystical experience — one he calls extrovertive and the other introvertive. It is important to realize that "the introvertive experience is wholly nonsensuous and nonintellectual." There is a sense of timelessness and spacelessness, of a dissolution of the sense of self, and a perfect unity of consciousness, devoid of any content. The extrovertive experience, however, "is sensory-intellectual in so far as it still perceives physical objects but is nonsensuous and nonintellectual in so far as it perceives them as 'all one." Both forms of mysticism share five criteria:

1. The mystical experience is noetic. It is neither a purely subjective nor a purely emotional experience but a real source of objective knowing.
2. The experience is ineffable and transcends the framework of reality which is describable in words.
3. The experience is sacred.

4. The experience is characterized by ecstatic feelings. It is a profoundly positive experience.
5. The experience defies logic. It is paradoxical (Stace, 1960:16-17).

We learned that extrovertive visionaries can talk about their experience. If you still doubt, their reports will teach you how to manifest visions in daily life.

❦ ❦ ❦

To round out the discussion, I want to clarify some terms which I have used at times interchangeably, though they are quite different by nature.

Mystical experiences seem to be the result of prolonged spiritual exercises, but, in most cases, mystical experiences are still spontaneous acts of grace. What is important is that when individuals come into the presence of the Source, they are fully conscious of the event and may spend a life time to communicate their profound experience (see, among others, Neihardt, 1961; Otto, 1957; Stace, 1960, and Underhill, 1955).

Ecstatic experiences seem to:

1. arise in a state of being beyond reason and self-control,
2. are accompanied by overwhelming emotions, esp. rapturous delight,
3. may lead to trance, esp. a mystic or prophetic trance (Webster, 1990:395).

This means that intense exaltation of mind and feelings may produce trances which lead to near immobility or provoke vehement expression and frenzied action.

Ecstasy seems to be the result of practitioners surrendering to the Divine Source, completely emerging themselves or feeling absorbed, without claiming the Source for themselves. It is important that ecstatics don't receive any other information as "being in the Light" (see, among others, Arbman, 1963-1970).

Peak experiences seem to be the result of heightened awareness. Faculties are mastered to perfection, intuitively, and without the detour of discursive thinking (e.g., during top performances, at sport events or other occasions of supernormal feats; see, among others, Maslow, 1964).

Visionary experiences seem to occur as the result of a search for the access to the Divine Source. Those who are looking for visionary experiences want to receive encouragement, nourishment, but mainly direction and information for their immediate, as well as, distant future (see, among others, Benz, 1982).

❦ ❦ ❦

Many before have invited and, in fact, keep inviting us to explore the Inner Source.

Jean Houston immediately comes to mind. She co-led the Human Capacity Program and has inspired many thousands in the United States and abroad for many years with the teachings of her Mystery School (see, e.g., 1987). Her inspiration evokes latent, unused creative forces and she "moves" her audiences so that they become active themselves.

And there is Rev. Lauren Artress, Canon for Special Ministries, who brought the dromenon (the labyrinth of Chartres) to San Francisco's Grace Cathedral. As Director of Quest, she offers church services where traditional concepts appear in a new light.

Don Campbell has already been teaching for decades toning and tuning. In his workshops and his books, he is opening the door for the exploration of sound (e.g., 1991, 1992).

Charles Tart wrote, among others, *Waking Up: Overcoming the Obstacles to Human Potential* (1986), adding new dimensions to science.

Norman Cousins said that, "Nothing is more powerful than an individual acting out of conscience, thus helping to bring the collective conscience to life" (1992:3). He asks us to discover our creativity and to find the source of healing, so that we become empowered. In sharing the newly gained insights selflessly, we serve not only ourselves but the "common good."

I am also evoking ecopsychology, a new branch of science which attempts "to span the gap between the personal and the planetary in a way that suggests political alternatives" (Roszak, 1992:18). And I call as witness Michael Murphy who in, *The Future of the Body*, speaks about synthesizing

> the facts of evolution with the extensive data related to extraordinary human functioning. It points toward a transcendent order of existence that works through evolution to unfold humanity's latent abilities. If metanormal abilities were realized by enough people, we might give birth to a revitalized civilization that honors the inner life, conserves energy, cares for the physical environment and invents new rituals of work and play (1992:7).

When Krishnamurti was asked to sum up his teachings, he replied, "I cannot help you." Indeed, we have to help ourselves.

II. Opening the Door

My Story

We have to become clear as glass so that the
Divine can shine through.

Meister Eckhart (1260 - 1327)

I have decided to tell my story because I want to share the process of seeing the Light. I want to talk about how and when I found the Source and why we have to continue the "process."

Daily chores tend to pull us away from the Center of Being, absorb our attention, and cloud our vision. Interconnecting is not a once-in-a-lifetime experience, it is a process of continually looking at ourselves and "all our relations." We easily forget that everything is "in flux."

When the American psychologist Mihaly Csikszentmihalyi studied a specific function he named "flow", he said

> it involves many human attributes, it clearly includes an exceptional type of volition. It is characterized, for example, by a marked concentration upon the activity at hand; by intrinsic motivation rather than a search for secondary benefits; by reduction or absence of limiting self-consciousness; by a pronounced sense of mastery; by highly efficient psycho-physical functioning; by positive moods; and by growth in complexity of the self. It breaks through to new levels of thought and behavior without social reinforcement, and perseveres without immediate rewards (in Murphy, 1992:140).

Motivated by this "exceptional type of volition," we have to investigate daily where we are and what we are doing. Are we striving for "mastery" or are we distracted by "secondary gains"? Do we penetrate the "complexity of self" and "break through to new levels of thought and behavior," without expecting "immediate rewards"? Do we stay in the "flow?"

I will report whatever comes to mind and not edit the "material." I will put into words what usually is not spelled out or, on first glance, may seem insignificant to others. I want to draw as accurate as possible a picture of my process. Knowing that nobody can escape subjectivity, I will take this fact into consideration as well. We need our ego to materialize and express inner experiences, but we should not forget that we are responsible for our materializations. That means, we should not hold on to our ego longer than necessary so that, after having accomplished its task, ego can merge again without leaving a trace.

⚜ ⚜ ⚜

Born on the fourth of November 1919 in Berlin, Germany, I stayed the first thirty-five years of my life in Europe. I went to America in 1955 and returned again to Germany in 1962 for another five-and-a-half years to take care of my dying parents. I also worked two full years (1971-1972 and 1978-1979) and several months in subsequent years in Asia. In 1994, I lived and worked altogether thirty-three years in the United States. Moving back and forth between continents, I feel as if I have lived at least seven different lives.

I grew up in a big metropolis at the crossroads of Europe, an only child, shy and withdrawn. (Sixty years later, I met the family who had lived in the apartment above us. They would not believe that the Heinzes' had a child. Not only was I never heard, I was also never seen by people who lived in the house where I grew up.)

My father and my mother fit the image of "good parents" who provide food, clothing, shelter, and teach proper behavior.

I remember that I began to search for what seemed to be missing, not knowing what I was looking for. I remember gazing at the small, triangular piece of sky, visible from one window of our third-floor apartment at the south end of a small courtyard.

I felt caressed by the wind and nourished by the songs of birds. I remember walking through cities painted golden by the evening sun on the billowing clouds.

At night, I listened to the fog horns of the freighters floating down the nearby river. I knew the Spree was flowing into the Havel, and the Havel into the Elbe, and the Elbe would finally merge with the North Sea and become part of the world oceans.

I was searching for the Unknown. I will always remember the following event:

> In summer, when I was still of preschool age, we used to go to a small coastal town at the Baltic Sea (Pomerania, now Poland). One day, I found myself standing alone on the beach.
>
> The sea touched the sky and I was breathing with the waves. I entered the rhythm of the waves and felt a sudden rush of energy as the sun, the wind, the sea were coursing right through me. I became the sun, the wind, and the sea. There was no "I" anymore, "I" had merged with everything else. A door had opened. All sensory perceptions — sounds, smells, tastes, shapes,

touches—melted into brilliant light. I became part of this pulsating energy.

This was the first time I experienced the "inter-con-nectedness" that seemed to be lacking in my daily life. Not only my mind and my body connected; my feelings and my soul reached out and became one with the Source. There was brilliant light, extreme joy, quiet rapture without excitement; peace and harmony. Nothing was static or crystallized in separate form. I felt the "Flow of Creation." Coming into life and dying were only transitions, the turning points in the Great Cycle of "Pulsating Being." (These are my words, seventy years later, at that time it was one "crystal clear," unified experience.)

When my parents called me, everything froze and returned to its "proper form." My parents thought I had a heat stroke and kept me in bed for a couple of days. Resting in the dark gave me time to return to consensus reality. I had stepped into a different reality where everything was whole and present. I had discovered a different level of consciousness but my culture was not prepared to help me process the experience.

Still a small child, I instinctively knew that the daily world I was living in had drawn curtains and was hiding the "truth." I could not talk about this experience but I felt grateful for and cherished this first encounter with the Source. It gave me the strength to go on.

Seventy years later, the book *Lame Deer—Seeker of Vision* fell into my hands. A Sioux medicine man was talking about a similar event:

> We Sioux believe that there is something within us that controls us, something like a second person almost. We call it nagi, what other people might call soul, spirit or essence. One can't see it, feel it or taste it, but that time on the hill [on his first vision guest when he was sixteen]—and only that once—I knew it was there inside of me. Then I felt the power surge through me like a flood. I cannot describe it, but it filled all of me (Erdoes, 1972:16).

When he was sixteen, he felt the "power surge" through him and each time afterwards, when he was seeking a vision, he would cry, "Wakan Tanka, Tunkashila, Onshimala...Grandfather Spirit, pity me, so that my people may live" (Erdoes, 1972:266).

Even now, seventy years later, every time I "interconnect," I remember the first experience which has become a measuring rod to test whether later "visions" are genuine. The message had been implicit the first time, but I only understood its meaning much later.

✵ ✵ ✵

I remember quite vividly how I first dealt with my fears and anxieties. It was customary in Germany to leave small children alone at night. The most fantastic ghost stories were told and then the child was put to bed, alone, in the dark. I pleaded with my parents to leave at least a light burning, but that would have been a waste of money. So the moment the bedroom door closed and darkness was all around me, the most hideous shapes arose from the corners of the room and began to move toward me. Not wanting to be "devoured," I screamed as loud as I could, for hours. As long as I screamed, they could not come closer. Neighbors began to complain about the noises coming from our apartment but my parents continued to leave me alone in the dark.

While marking my territory with my voice, I felt safe and the ghosts seemed, indeed, to respect the power of my vocal cords. However, I could not keep this up forever. Exhausted from hours of crying every evening, I had to stop. I was desperate, not knowing what to do. But then, I remember it clearly, it suddenly occurred to me that it could be my fear that was creating all these monsters. The moment this thought came to me, the ghosts disappeared, the spell was broken. This was my first lesson on what we create with our thoughts. Since then, I check "reality"—what I see and perceive—by shifting my attention to a different mode. Looking at what transpires in or outside of us from different angles, changes the "picture."

I also frequently felt left out and had the urge to escape this isolation. I wanted to break out of the vicious circle of victimization. I realized that I was dependent on my parents who took perfect care of my body but treated me like an object. Somehow I must have accepted the fact of being left to my own resources and never developed enough bitterness to shun human contact, on the contrary, communication became the reason to live.

(When people call me a "lone wolf," they forget that we need some time each day to be alone and contemplate on "all our connections.")

The earliest memory of refusing to be kept out goes back to the time when I was less than a year old. (I wonder why this image has stayed with me in all its details now for nearly seventy-four years). I stood in my crib against the south wall of my parents' bedroom. To the right there was a white Dutch-tile oven which we never used, not even in winter. Another green Dutch-tile oven stood in the adjoining living roam and we would leave the door open when we went to bed. (Germans like to sleep in the cold. I still sleep with open windows, even in winter). The crib faced my parents' beds. Right and left of their beds stood two night stands with small lamps on beautifully embroidered mats. In the northwest corner was a commode with a wash basin which nobody used because we had a portable wash stand in the kitchen. The walls of the bedroom were covered with green wallpaper on which ornaments in different shades of green were painted. I could not yet walk or talk. Supposed to sleep after lunch, I was not sleepy at all. The sun was shining through the white-cloud curtains and I heard the voices of my parents in the distance. I was left out of something.

I still remember the tall rungs of the railing around the crib. I tried to get out, by pulling myself up again and again; then my memory blacked out. Later, my mother told me that, as a very small child, I had suddenly appeared in the kitchen and they never could figure out how I had gotten out of the crib with its tall wooden railing; and how I had managed to crawl over sixty feet through the bedroom, the living room and a long hall to the kitchen (the doors had been left open, but I had to move them to get through). My intent must have pushed me into a different state of consciousness which gave me the strength to express myself.

There are other memories of being isolated, put up on high chairs, without my toys. My mother rarely played with me and would not allow me to play with other children or let me play by myself. She had told me to sit still because she had work to do. I saw her looking at me and laughing about my frustration. I was held captive by the high chair. It did not make any sense and, from this time on, I began to look for ways to circumvent unnecessary restrictions and obstructions in the future.

I am reporting these emotions only to show that early frustrations need not necessarily have negative consequences. Obstacles strengthened my intent and my survival instinct drove me early to overcome barriers again and again wherever I went. I founded literary circles (the Group of Twelve, a young writers' group) in post-World War II Berlin; literary salons; and a theater group (Art Repertory Theater) in the San Francisco Bay Area in the sixties. I founded the Asian Folklore Studies Group with 945 scholars in the United States and 11 countries in Europe and Asia, and Independent Scholars of Asia, Inc., with 172 members (123 in 34 of the United States and 49 in 23 Asian countries). Both groups attempt to raise hope in as many people as possible and promote Asian thought in non-Asian countries. I have been producing the "Universal Dialogue" series in the San Francisco Bay Area since the seventies, and have called the annual International Conference on the Study of Shamanism and Alternate Modes of Healing since 1984. The main goals are to tie different networks together and to touch as many individuals as possible, assisting those who need encouragement until they are ready to work on their own. After planting the seed and nourishing the first growth, I move on to whomever and whatever crosses my way. I do not attempt to "save the world." I see myself as a "candle-bearer" or a St. Bernard with the little flask of reviving liquid.

I never allowed anybody, e.g., professors at the University of California, Berkeley, to break my spirit, and I fought those who put up artificial barriers on their own grounds. But I get ahead of myself, so let us return to my early childhood.

Educated to obey without questioning, I had to display acceptable behavior. In the world of the twenties, there seemed to be nobody who could teach me to compensate for the "emptiness" in daily life. There was nobody to tell me "why I had been cut off."

I never questioned the authority of my parents. I soon learned, for example, that whatever toys they gave me, my mother had already promised to one of my numerous cousins. I was not allowed to play with them so that they would remain in good condition and could be given away at any time. My mother also used to buy dozens of chocolate bars (a rare sight for me) and distributed them to visiting cousins. I knew already, she was always one bar short: mine. Dozens of children were munching chocolate around me, telling me how fortunate I was to have chocolate every day. I kept my mouth shut and was not resentful. I must have recognized early the priorities in my life. Much later, Buddhism acknowledged that it is helpful not to get attached to material things. There was really no reason to complain!

I cherished my "dreams" and tried to bring their pulsating energy into the reality of the day. Visions and dreams kept me alive and gave me the strength not to be swayed by the imbalances in my daily life. Though I stayed vulnerable and sensitive, I did not become bitter or belligerent. It would have added more imbalances to what was out of balance already.

Books supplied some nourishment. They told me what other people had accomplished in their life and assured me that I also could try when the time was right. I went to the library daily to check out at least two books. The librarian was skeptical about my voracious reading but I could tell her every time what I had found in the books and what I still was looking for.

Fortunately, at that time, my parents bought a piano. It was a status symbol. I hated the piano lessons with teachers who did not know how to inspire children, but when I was alone, I played the piano or began to listen to music on the radio. I found that sound has the power to attune and does establish the longed-for "connection." As often as possible, I played the piano or turned on the radio. The sound of a flute sustained my longing for the Source and prevented my crash landing in a hostile material world. Classical harpsichord music supported the flow of thoughts when I was writing and the music of Mozart was always healing and elevating. He had transformed the tragedies in his life into triumphant, joyful dances. I rejoiced with him. And I howled with the recorded voices of wolves, to declare my independence.

I began to experiment with sounds to find which one would meet the needs of the moment. The musical discoveries led naturally to movement. Yes, I could dance what needed to be expressed. Dance, one of the most pleasant experiences in the material world, allowed me to discover muscles I did not know I had. And, during the hilariously exhausting dances, the hidden Source of Energy would emerge.

In other words, I practiced listening first, and then I allowed my whole body to become involved and tuned. Everything was moving. I danced until all frustrations and anxieties were gone. (The therapeutic value of music, movement and dance has now become more widely known, see Campbell, 1991, 1992). Since that time, I have consciously used music and dance for myself, with my students and clients, and whenever else appropriate in my relationships. In moving, we find release and are encouraged to express ourselves.

At that time, I also overcame my fear of water, i.e., I recognized the obstacle which had prevented me from swimming. After weeks of failing miserably and sinking to the bottom like a stone, my teacher told me that I never would learn to swim and suggested I should give up. The magic word was "Never." The next time, I swam for half an hour. My determination overruled my fears. This was the second time I understood that we have to surrender our fears and anxieties first to receive what we are looking for. How liberating it was to find out that the moment I surrendered, the water was ready to embrace me. The "oceanic feeling," once experienced in the womb of my mother and four years later during the mystical experience at the sea, reinforced my memories of the Source. Water is always ready to caress and support us.

Later, my mother explained my childhood nightmares of drowning and being swallowed by giant waves. When she had been bathing me as a small child, she had inadvertently held my head under water. Knowing that I could swim, the nightmares of drowning stopped. (I still swim forty minutes daily to allow imbalances to dissolve and to experience the invigorating embrace of the water.)

To strengthen my spine, our house doctor suggested that I should take up rowing and my parents surprisingly allowed me to join the rowing team of my high school. (Having the right "posture" was important to them.) I could have taken a bus, but I walked over two hours each time from our apartment in Charlottenburg to the boat house at the Stoessensee (great lake west of Berlin). It was a pilgrimage, a cherished preparation for the rowing experience which allowed me to glide over the chain of lakes surrounding Berlin. My pent-up energy went into the rhythmic movement of the oars. Through this new opening I could break out of the mold and feel liberated. Caressed by water and wind, I enjoyed moving with the water and the wind. Swans would fiercely attack us because they felt challenged by our boat. Our oars kept them away and we decided to respect and admire each other from afar. We had joined the flow.

I will never forget the big storm which caught up with us on the Wannsee (a big lake west of Berlin). I had to steer our boat across large waves underneath the connecting line of two moving big freighters. The tension grew. At this point, I interconnected. During these rare moments of complete interconnection, which is nothing but fine tuning while going with the flow, discursive thoughts have no place. Any thought would be fatal, because it introduces the possibility of doubt.

I once walked on skis over an icy tree placed across a gorge in the Sudeten Mountains. Nobody with a sound mind would dare to do this. Later I read about "trance walking," the Tibetan lung-gom. Gom means "meditation" and lung "signifies both the elementary state of 'air'...as well as the subtle vital energy or psychic force" (Govinda, 1977:81). When everything is connected, our whole body moves without thinking, carried by the feeling of oneness. (We can reach this state in emergencies or through intense meditation training which makes it possible to recall the state from memory.)

Another such point of interconnection occurred when the bells of the village churches in a Sudeten valley rang in the New Year and we, holding lighted torches, skied down the surrounding mountains, writing trails of light into the snow. The light we were carrying united with the sound of the bells, celebrating the New Year. Lama Anagarika Govinda speaks of the "foretaste of what every human being can attain to when he realizes the dormant powers of light, which are buried like seeds deep within his soul" (1977:8).

Evoking the Source of Energy gave me the strength not to become confused by outside events. We encounter many situations we cannot identify with and ignorance seems to close in on us, but this ignorance needs not get under our skin. Body, emotions, mind and soul need not separate, they can dance together. Facing ignorance gives us the opportunity to shed some light into the dark.

Consensus reality took care of my "grounding." My confirmation into the Lutheran faith, for example, brought up some traumatic aspects. I had gone to Sunday school for over a year, hungry for some divine clues, but what we learned in church resembled what we learned at school. We repeated words without fully understanding their meaning.

My history teacher and, later, my math teacher were the exceptions. They first kindled my desire for exploring the past, including archaeology. (Forty years later I excavated an Indian mound in Grass Valley, California, and I am still seeking historical sites where the sacred has manifested in the past). My math teacher satisfied my passion for logical thinking. I was even allowed to do my homework during class because I was so bored by the repetitions for slower students. In exchange I had to tutor my classmates in mathematics. But let's get back to my confirmation.

Although he had been the minister for the last German emperor some sixteen years ago, my pastor had stayed humble and understanding. He was a good man, but I had problems with the Christian dogma. As a child, I had tried to sit in church in a place where I wasn't forced to see the crucifix on the altar. I was horrified by the agony of a man who allegedly had died for me. Under no circumstances did I ever want anybody to die for me, especially not under such terrible circumstances. (Fifty years later, Asians told me that they never could understand why Westerners worship a crucified god. In other words, why Westerners are so fixated on suffering).

Shortly before my confirmation, I went to my pastor and told him that I could not be confirmed because the doctrine of original sin was unacceptable to me. I deserved punishment for what I had done, but I could not accept blame for something I hadn't. When God created Adam and Eve, the Garden of Eden and the Tree with the infamous apple, didn't he know that Adam and Eve would e at the apple? How could an omniscient god punish mankind for the temptation he had created himself? I refused to believe that I was born in sin because my parents were married and I had been baptized. I could not promise to go to a church each Sunday where such beliefs were upheld. My pastor told me how much he appreciated my honesty, but suggested I should go through with the confirmation for my parents' sake, not to cause unnecessary commotion. God knew and he knew what I was thinking, so there would be no dishonesty involved. He added that God likes those who are searching for the truth and prefers them to those who simply do lip service.

Well, he convinced me to "play the game," but when it came to the blessing, I slid down from the cushion on which we were kneeling so that the pastor's hands could not touch me. I did not want any undeserved blessing. The pastor bent down deeply, but I was on the floor already. The rest of the day I could not help crying. Everybody thought I was overwhelmed by the experience. What did they know? To make things worse, an orchestra appeared and played a famous tune which, in English translation, was the equivalent to "youth is beautiful, it is now over. It never will return." If this meant that the best time of my life was over, "they" certainly could have it. The rest was another flood of tears.

My mother had arranged a big confirmation, with endless house cleaning, cooking and baking. The large number of guests had been asked to give money instead of presents. The money would be used for my education. After the celebration, I inquired about the money and my mother informed me that the celebration had been very costly. I don't know what was going through my mind; all I knew was that my frustrations boiled down to plain anger. This whole "farce" had gone too far. If the money was not being used for my education, I insisted on getting at least something to remind me of that "memorable day." So my mother bought me a handbag so ugly that I never wore it. I also got five marks with which I bought the piano score of the Peer Gynt Suite by Grieg. "Correctness," even in small things, was and still is, very important to me.

My mother found that studying at a university would be a nuisance. "Teachers only want money. You will marry and then all the money is wasted." I fought four days and nights but wound up in a commercial college to learn "more marketable skills." I loathed learning to type and to keep books, but the parental advice has "paid off" over time. When I needed money, I could work as a secretary, and I am now my own secretary, which saves a lot of time, energy, and even money. Responsive to the speed of my thoughts, the computer has now become an indispensable tool.

When I turned eighteen, I became financially independent and worked as a secretary for the rector of the University of Berlin, next to the City Castle, the State Opera House and the prestigious Avenue of Unter den Linden. I had wanted to study chemistry and biology to explore the secrets of life, but work-study or scholarships were not possible at that time. Neither I nor my father wanted to join the Nazi party.

After a few months, a party leader showed up with one of his protégées and I was demoted to work in the registrar's office. This prompted me to enter the Arbeitsdienst (Labor Service) voluntarily.

For half a year, I worked with peasants in the country. Sometimes the farms were miles away from our camp, so I had to ride a bicycle. After having catapulted several times out of narrow ruts on the country road, I began to enjoy bicycling through nature. I remember stopping on the way with the others and raiding the fruit trees alongside the road. Once a policeman almost caught us, but each of us grabbed the next bicycle and we escaped. When the policeman asked the farmers in our village who had been late for work, everyone pretended we had already been working for hours (the fruit trees belonged to the other village). At noon, we then went around and located our own bicycles. There had been such an abundance of frui t that we felt we had not deprived anybody of anything. We loved the land we were working on.

For a while I had to cook for a group of ten men. My knowledge of cooking was limited because my mother never had allowed me to cook. If I started to prepare some food, she would go into such endless stories about how to do it "right" that I dropped the idea of learning cooking from her. Now I had to resort to scientific memories. Potatoes and vegetables apparently needed boiling, which meant you clean and put them in a pot of water to be placed on the open fire on the hearth. The cooking process was complicated by another task. I had to clean three large stalls with fifty geese each and the three flocks did not like each other. Every time a door was not closed properly, they would start a war of Trojan dimensions. You would see me in the midst of one hundred fifty geese, separating them by getting hold of their long necks and throwing them into their proper stalls. However, I did not always throw the right goose into the right stall.

For the cooking, I had to recall experiments from my chemistry class. Alkaline would soften substances, so I put some baking soda into the boiling vegetables. When we do this to red cabbage, it takes on an ugly green color. Nobody would eat something that looked like the turd of a cow. But then I recalled that acid turns litmus paper red. Vinegar! There was, however, no vinegar at hand and I had to dispatch a runner to the village. He returned just in time with the bottle of vinegar high in his right hand. Having, in the meantime, defended the pot from hungry men, I poured the vinegar into the cabbage. It dutifully developed a pleasant red color, and everybody was delighted with the results. I mention these episodes to illustrate how I enjoyed the exploration of new fields and how I got satisfaction out of applying deductive thought to courageous experiments.

Then, in 1939, the war broke out and I had to stay a couple of months longer, I was transferred to a former men's camp outside of Berlin. I remember entering the sauna at night and then diving into the snow outside. The heat-dissolved all grievances and the fresh snow brought our energies to the surface.

Harvesting potatoes on my knees for days and weeks was not easy, but it felt good to dig the bulbs out of the earth with our bare hands. I felt part of the natural process of planting, growing, and harvesting.

I remember going to the dairy farm, accompanied by a beautiful dog that had adopted us. I could not prevent the dog from chasing chickens and he finally killed the rooster of the dairy owner. The dog then followed me through the small town, proudly displaying his catch in his mouth. (He, obviously, had been trained as a hunting dog.) Shortly after, the dog disappeared and I was told that it had been shot. For some time, I felt responsible for not preventing its early demise.

Returning from the Labor Service (Arbeitsdienst), I was asked to assist foreign visitors, because I spoke several foreign languages. I remember meeting Sven Hedin, the great Asian explorer. He waited patiently in my office before I recognized him. I also remember refusing to work for Bengt Berg, well known for protecting wildlife but overbearing in his attitude to others. Not used to having services denied him, he shouted that I never would get any books from him and broke a glass door for which the German government had to pay. (The door was not deducted from my salary.) I could not tolerate unreasonable behavior.

On my vacations, I explored Germany, hiking through the Harz Mountains, looking from the Wartburg over the land and paying my respects to Weimar and Jena, the cities of Goethe and Schiller. I explored the castles and vineyards of the Rhine and Mosel rivers in the west, and visited the cities of Danzig and Koenigsberg in East Prussia, where I followed an elk down the Nougat. The images of these treasures belong now to a past that has been reinterpreted by shifts in population. I would like to revisit some of these sites to experience their transformations, especially the castle of the German Knights at Marienwerder. I firmly believe that essence survives the vagaries of politics. We experience awe wherever Spirit has manifested, be it in a cathedral, a synagogue, a mosque, a sacred grove or a sacred mountain. Christian cathedrals have been built on sites of earlier indigenous rituals. This raises the question of what will be built on the ruins of churches torn down throughout America (because congregations can no longer support them)? High-rise bank buildings?

Around that time, I was in love with a young man whom I had met at a theater group. We phoned and exchanged letters and poems daily (mail in Berlin was, in 1940, delivered three times a day). I waited six years for my lover to return from World War II and imprisonment in the United States. When I saw him again, I realized that he had become a homosexual. I decided to keep him as a friend; obviously he could not be the father of my children.

I have now many children, though none of them grew in my womb. When people talk about their "own" children, I wonder whether we ever "own" anybody or anything. My childlessness is voluntary. When World War II finally ended, eligible men were married already or had died in the war. I did meet another man who could have become the father of my children, but I learned in time that he was married already. For a while, I considered raising a child as a single mother, but this would have meant giving up the work in which I had become involved. I did not want to be a half-time mother.

Isn't it irresponsible to put another human being into an increasingly overpopulated and unsafe world? Isn't it more important to direct efforts toward the many who need motherly love, understanding, assistance? There are so many souls who need help. There are more "children" to nurture than I physically can produce. Parenting came naturally to me.

However, I warned myself early not to become a devouring mother. I had to explore what needs my "children" had. What was necessary for their survival? Encouragement? Nourishment? And then comes always the point when we have to let "our children" go. We have to learn how to let go at the right time.

It is such a joy to see children grow and I use the word "children" in the widest sense possible. There are adults who lost contact with themselves. They don't trust anybody and, what is worse, they don't trust themselves anymore. They need support so that they are not crushed by adverse winds. Teaching and acting are two professions where strong motherly feelings can be expressed, and, in both cases, we can see immediate results. We activate the faculties of others, becoming catalysts for crippled souls. We wake them up, like a mother wakes her children every morning so they won't be late for school.

People are afraid of moving. And what is worse, they are not ready to listen either. We have to attract their attention. We have to involve them playfully in useful scenarios. And, in using a symbolic language, we create rituals to lead them to a place outside of ordinary time and space where the unexpected can occur. Staying in the middle of the stream, we assist others to get to the "water." The drinking they have to do themselves.

But let's get back to the sequence of events in my life. Dissatisfied with my administrative job, I saved money to train as an actress. I wanted to learn how to communicate more effectively. I had entered the path toward liberation and needed to share my experiences and insights more effectively.

I failed the entrance exam but passed the second exam with flying colors and began to study with a famous actress. For two years, I worked in an office during the day but got up early in the morning and went to the park behind the Charlottenburg Palace, where I rehearsed my roles, walking around the lake when nature rose from the night. I soaked up the energies around me and used them in my roles. This was a time when I did not need much sleep.

Studying different roles, I gave expression to the other women inside of me. (We all seem to be multiple personalities and only those who cannot control their imagery need help). Playing tragic, as well as, comical roles, I could explore different aspects of being. I could express my pain about the death of a friend or relative in a dramatic scene and offer a catharsis to those in the audience who had suffered a similar loss. As my inhibitions dissolved and my sensitivity increased, I also learned to use more humor in my everyday relationships. Becoming vulnerable in a protected environment, I learned to transcend the barriers between the inner and outer world more easily. From the time rehearsals began until the day of performance in front of an audience, I explored my potentials and became more fully involved in the growing number of interconnections.

During the bombing of Berlin, my teacher evacuated to Dresden and I took the train to stay with her for a few days as often as possible. Sometimes, I was allowed to appear as an extra on the Dresden stage. I remember standing in the wings and watching the transformations of famous actors. One day I was thrown from the stage because I had danced too wildly as a witch during the Walpurgisnacht in Goethe's "Faust." (Even witches had to maintain decorum on the Dresden cultural scene). I failed the final exam in Dresden because there had been professional fights between drama teachers, but I passed the second final in great style in front of actors of the Wiener Burgtheater (Viennese Court Theater).

I had learned about the date of the second final exam only one day ahead of time and had to take the night train from Berlin to Vienna. Standing at a train window, I repeated my twelve leading roles and several shorter sequences of other plays. In Vienna, I went straight to the classical building where we were supposed to perform. I had to wait for hours. I was the second to last to be called on stage.

Tiredness had begun to take hold of my body; nevertheless, I went right into a dramatic scene from "Di Braut von Messina" (The Bride of Messina) by Schiller. It was the scene where a mother finds her son dead and cries out in pain. A Viennese actress (Charlotte Wolters) had become famous with this scene and it occurred to me that it might not be wise to challenge Viennese actors, but it was too late to change. The tiredness had removed any mental obstacles and I allowed the role to en-trance me. My second choice was another classical play by Schiller, *Mary Stuart.* I selected the scene where Queen Elizabeth contemplates the signing of Mary

Stuart's death sentence, using a modern approach, low key but intense.

Then I waited silently on the stage while the examiners kept talking to each other. I had the right to two electives; now the committee had to decide what else they wanted me to perform. After a while, I heard a voice saying, "Why don't you come down?" Convinced I had failed, I planted myself in front of the committee's table and, with my last drop of energy, demanded to know whether I had passed or not. I had been on my feet for forty-eight hours and could not stand any uncertainty anymore. Exhausted as I was, I must have looked very funny, because they broke out in laughter and somebody said, "Of course, you have passed." I stumbled out of the hall. A friend tried to console me by saying "You can repeat the exam." She took my tiredness for depression and was surprised when I suddenly shouted, "What are you talking about, I passed!"

Then I ran out into the city. My tiredness was gone. The whole day I roamed around in Vienna. I tasted wine in Grinzing and managed to get a ticket for the Wiener Burgtheater that night. It was standing room only. After a while, I had to step out into the vestibule where an usher silently offered me a glass of water. Tiredness finally had taken its toll.

I still remember my first public appearance. After long rehearsals, the day before the performance in a large theater with over three thousand seats, my stomach turned inside out. Do we have to get rid of impurities before we create? Why had I ever become an actress? I would die, drowned by the laughter of three thousand people who would discover my incompetence on first glance. I did not even remember my first line, but somehow managed the fifty steps to the center of the stage. Fainting seemed to be the only escape. But then the spotlights hit me and the monster with the many thousand eyes was holding its breath, ready to strike. "Somebody" started to talk. It was not me. "It" talked through me, using my vocal cords. There was no other sound. Was the audience still there? Time seemed to have stopped. And then, the wave of attention reached me, the audience had joined in the "dance" and "we" were carried to unknown heights. It was a perfect wedding night. We interconnected!

❧ ❧ ❧

When World War II broke out in Europe, I was eighteen. The army drafted relatives and friends. Some died on the battlefields, some in air raids. The war drew our attention away from spiritual pursuits. Hitler had tightened his grip on Germany. I will never forget the marches of the storm troopers when Hitler came to power on January 30, 1933 and I was thirteen. The glowing fire of the storm troopers' torches, snaking through the streets, carried the message of approaching doom. Six and a half years later, the terror had materialized and anybody who showed dissatisfaction was executed, within days.

We learned caution, carefully choosing who we spoke with and what we talked about. The theater offered a safety valve, because it allowed suppressed emotions and thoughts to manifest. Actors spoke the words of the author; however, the way we spoke them conveyed a content beyond literal meaning. My body, my feelings, my mind and my soul felt liberated during the performance and the audience felt liberation, too.

The bombing of Berlin began in November 1942, when I turned twenty-three. For two-and-a-half years, we were attacked by air up to five times each day and up to five times each night. We had to come to terms with death. I had to choose between being destroyed or destroying myself (suicide), becoming insane or completely numb. None of these alternatives felt right. So I evoked Death and Death materialized. We "talked." I felt the awesome presence of all the forms in the world, dying and being born, in constant change. I surrendered, taking Death into my body. Each part of my body got icy cold and numb, one by one. I experienced the process of dying in my body, mind, emotions, and soul. Then the coldness turned into a flame that burned all residue. I stepped out of the flame like a tool that had been steeled in the fire. In surrendering to Death, my mortal fears had disappeared.

Knowing Death was present all the time was like signing a contract. We fear the process of dying because we forget that we begin to die the moment we materialize, i.e., are born, and enter Infinite Life at the moment of dematerialization, i.e., death. During the period between these two transitions, we have to accept our responsibilities in the material world. I was now ready for this task and promised to help the living, as well as, the dying in the service of Death.

The heightened awareness of Death saved my life. One evening, for example, I had not been able to reach the air raid shelter and remained at an entrance to a locked building. I could see the bombs falling. Since they were released from high-flying planes, several minutes passed before they hit the ground. Suddenly, I left the scant protection the entrance niche had offered me and, disregarding the rain of falling shrapnel from the anti-air-raid guns, ran out on the street. The moment I reached the next building, the house where I had stood a few seconds earlier was hit by a large bomb and completely blown to pieces.

For twelve years (1933-1945), we lived between paranoia and inner peace for which we had created a space deep inside of us, fluctuating back and forth. Inhuman events tried to overwhelm us. The question whether the terror would ever end had to be dealt with. After another assassination attempt on Hitler in 1944, the war still did not end and the killing of millions of people continued.

Only those who have lived in a country with a destructive government know the baring of the soul when human dignity is put to the ultimate test. At night we would hear the bombs hitting the buildings around us. Bombs were dropped in a series of three. If the first one hit close by, we could be sure the other two would hit farther away, but when the first one hit far away, it was possible that the second or third could hit the spot where we waited underground. Would we live through the next minute?

Hundreds, no, thousands of people in the city of Berlin with four and a half million people died slowly in the provisional air raid shelters underneath their houses, crushed during the collapse of buildings and burned by fire from incendiary bombs. Or they were caught in the fire storms which swept through the streets. Unspeakable terror prevailed. There was death on a massive scale, inside and outside the concentration camps. Berlin became a pile of rubble. The smell of burning flesh permeated the air. One day, I saw a human hand on the sidewalk. I was walking through human dust; nothing else remained of that human being.

We left our home in the morning, carrying backpacks with our most precious belongings. We never knew whether we would see each other or our home again. My country was being destroyed—physically, emotionally, morally and spiritually—piece by piece, and the social fabric became threadbare and torn.

But amidst death and destruction, something surprisingly human began to blossom. We helped each other. We put out the fires in neighboring houses. We saved each other's belongings, sometimes it was a bird cage with a bird that had already died of shock, sometimes an empty violin case. What mattered was that those who suffered knew they were not alone. I never will forget an old emaciated man who suddenly appeared in front of me in a still burning house and insisted that I drink a cup of coffee. He offered me the ration he had saved for a special day because I had salvaged some of his belongings. After fifty years, I still see this cup of coffee—a symbol of humanity.

I waited for a sign to convince myself that I should survive. Why did the Christian God I had been introduced to allow such atrocities? Didn't he have the power to intervene? Looking for something tangible to hold on to, something that would connect the past with the future, I found a petrified sea urchin I had picked up on one of the beaches of the Baltic Sea when I was a child. It had survived thousands, if not millions, of years. It was perfectly preserved in its essence. This stone provided the metaphor for survival. My body could be destroyed (and, at that time, death would have been a relief), but the essence could not be touched. So I put everything of my culture—Bach, Beethoven, great painters, poets and philosophers—into this stone. I held the stone in my hand when I faced death in the air raid shelters. I held the stone in my hand when I learned about the atrocities in the concentration camps, by word of mouth (to speak about it was punished by death). The horror had to end some day or I would die holding this stone in my hand. This stone contained the essence of what is German. When Jews and Germans together can wash the atrocities from this stone with their tears, then a real healing can take place. I made a vow that, should I survive, I would never again tolerate the perversion of the human mind under whatever circumstances.

In 1945, the Russian Army surrounded Berlin which became a war zone. I began to work in hospitals. Fourteen-year-old boys had been drafted into the army in an attempt to save the lost cause, as well as sixty-year-old men who cried for their mother, their wife, their children. I took them into my arms and tried to rock them into a gentle death.

❦ ❦ ❦

I was twenty-five when Hitler's reign and the horrors of World War II finally came to an end, but peace was not as pleasant as we had hoped. We could not understand why the Americans did not liberate Berlin. They stopped at the river Elbe and allowed the Russians to occupy our city. This meant eight days of plunder and rape of any female—from young girls to eighty-year-old women.

Starvation continued for another year. We lived on rations less than 1,000 calories a day (one slice of bread, a pinch of salt in hot water to fill the stomach). We ate grass cooked like spinach and boiled the bark of trees. I went mushroom hunting where Russians kept their horses. I was half the weight I am now. (The American air lift to feed Berlin during the "blockade" brought some relief and we blessed the American soldiers who risked their lives.)

We were culturally starved, too. Long before the big theaters could be rebuilt, any suitable building was converted into a theater or concert hall. These cultural oases were filled to capacity each evening. I enjoyed being an actress.

My first one-year contract brought me to the town of Waren (Mecklenburg), where I stayed in an architect's house, directly on the shores of the huge Lake Muritz. After the performance, most of the actors would come home with me and we swam, naked, in the lake, spearing crabs under the moon, and enjoying the peace. Afterwards we raided the owner's large orchard for apples and pears and then cooked the crabs in my room. We would discuss world affairs freely.

The next year, I went from Waren to Neustrelitz, where I played classical and comical roles and recited Prokofiev's "Peter and the Wolf" against a large orchestra which tried to drown my voice. Unsuccessfully, I must say, because my voice had been strong since early childhood. My mother told me when well-minded people would look into my crib, they were up for a surprise. I would sound out their intentions and either answer with a big smile or, sensing negativity, protest loudly. Once my mother thought I had protested unjustly, but the woman turned out to be a hypocrite later on. As I had kept ghosts away with my voice as a small child, I was trying to keep negative people away too. My voice has been my protector bolstering my self-trust and self-worth from an early age on.

Encounters with approaching Death continued. In 1949, I went from Neustrelitz to Guben where I "played" in a theater close to the Polish border. Because performances were scheduled during the holidays, I could not join my family in Berlin. So I lit a candle and turned on the radio. One station was broadcasting Bruch's violin concerto. Captured by the music, I did not remember undressing and going to bed—I entered different stages of consciousness. When I awoke in the morning, I still felt weightless, peaceful and interconnected with the universe. I realized that something had happened and that I had to write it down.

> I was walking through a large house that looked like a shelter for people wanting to rest on their journey, like a refugee camp. I pinched myself to find out whether I was dreaming but I felt the pain. While I was wandering through long floors, I saw many rooms, right and left, but all the doors were closed. I cannot remember whether I actually saw a human shape or just heard a human voice which told me I could not stay. There was no room for me. Not yet.

> I was given a basket which one would use to collect fruit. Something was moving inside the basket. It was a red cat, purring and waiting to be caressed. As soon as I touched the cat, the house, the basket, and the cat disappeared, and I saw a large garden in front of me.

The garden was on a slope, bordering a lake or river. People were walking up and down, talking to each other in soft voices. It sounded like the murmuring of a spring or the purring of a cat. The people wore timeless gowns of a grayish color. Under the blinding sun, all colors in the garden seemed to fade away. Through the bright haze, a man left the crowd and walked toward me. He was an uncle, the brother of my mother. I had always liked him because he had a cheerful and giving personality. While he was talking to me, I realized that all the other people in the garden had already died. I recognized dead friends, relatives, and neighbors. At the same moment, I also remembered that my uncle and I were the only living beings in the garden. There was nothing unnatural about it. I pressed my thumbnail against the palm of my hand and again felt pain.

When I asked my uncle why we were in this garden, he led me to a building to the left, which looked like a mausoleum. We entered and I saw two sarcophagi. A neighbor who had been close to me when I was a child was resting in one of them. My uncle began to lie down in the other. I asked him why. He had talked to me so freely before and continued to move his lips, but I could not hear a sound. It was like being under water where we can see but all noise s are blunted. While I was trying to understand him and make myself understood, I woke up from the effort.

I wrote down what I remembered and put the report into an envelope, which I sealed and gave to a colleague, asking him to open it only on request.

Rehearsals and performances asked for my full attention, so I forgot the experience. Six weeks later, when we were having lunch at the theater's cafeteria, the mail was distributed. There was a letter from my parents. My actor friend asked me why I was so quiet and I told him to open the sealed envelope. Then I gave him my parents' letter. They wrote that the neighbor who had been lying in one of the sarcophagi had died at the time I had seen him that night, and that my uncle, with whom I had spoken, had been rushed to the hospital where he had died three weeks later. I had responded to the thoughts of dying people who had not been "on my mind" in consensus reality. Contacting me seemed to have eased their transition — they felt released.

When the political situation in the Eastern Zone worsened, I did not renew my contract and went back to West Berlin, starting a writer's group (Group of the Twelve) and organizing literary readings and performances.

I crossed two borders (the border between Berlin and the Russian zone and the border between the Russian and the American zone) four times to visit a cousin in Munich. First, I went with a man who terrified me by suddenly displaying a gun. We could be shot immediately crossing the area closed off with electric wires and land mines. We also had to be aware of dogs the East German guards would release. The second time, I went alone and got lost in a swamp. Looking up, I recognized the constellation of Orion and calculated the direction I had to walk by figuring out how much Orion would move during the night. From that time on, I have had a special relationship with the Big Hunter in the sky.

During one trip from West Germany back to the enclave of West Berlin, I was arrested at the Potsdam border and asked to surrender my Eastern passport. I did not carry it with me, so the guards asked for my wrist watch and let me go. They thought I would not return. However, I felt I had not committed any crime, collected my Eastern passport in West Berlin and went back to the Eastern border, demanding my watch. The guard grudgingly returned it but ordered that I should be taken to the Potsdam Prison.

When we walked through the streets and I sat in the bus, next to the grim-looking guard, the faces of the people around me showed that they knew I was about to meet an unknown fate. In the prison, guards on the tower even looked into the stalls of the bathrooms. When I learned that people on the benches, right and left, had been sitting there for several days, waiting for a hearing, I knew I had to do something fast. So I went into the next room and politely asked the interrogating official to be released. I had voluntarily come back and surrendered my passport. Now I had to return to Berlin because my parents would worry if I did not come back at a reasonable time. The official was so surprised at my audacity that he told me to go. I insisted on an escort because I did not want to be arrested again without the right papers. So he laughed and told a guard to bring me to the next rapid-train station. The guard smuggled me into the station, because I did not have any Eastern money and he did not have sufficient money either to buy a ticket from East Germany to West Berlin.

When the train finally reached a West Berlin station, I was relieved and leaned against the window. When I woke up, I was again on the other side, in East Berlin.

Fortunately, it was a station where trains to West Berlin stopped on the same platform. I was very careful not to fall asleep again in the train to West Berlin.

I mention these events only so you can understand how it felt living in a divided country.

After the currency reform, the economic miracle in Germany became visible. Parts of Berlin were still in rubble; however, our hard work, starting from scratch, unbending nails and cleaning bricks, was showing results.

We could fly out of Berlin and visit foreign countries. So I spent three summers in Italy, traveling on a monthly ticket up and down from Milan to Sicily and back. I only had to go to the next station and jump on the Express train to be carried to St. Marco in Venice, to Padua, Ravenna, the arena of Verona, the Etruscan catacombs of Orvieto and Spoleto. In Sienna, I visited the simple hut of St. Francis of Assisi where the doves still talk to him. I stood in awe in front of Michelangelo's Moses in San Pietro in Vincoli in Rome. Walking back through history, the signs of persecution of Christians who hid in the catacombs contrasted with the beauty of Vatican City. Forgotten were the inquisition's persecutions of non-believers. Through the blast of the midday sun, hundreds of homeless cats climbed over marble headstones in the cemetery outside Rome where Goethe's son, August, had found his resting place.

I watched Florence rising from the morning fog. History became alive—Dante's house, the Doors of Paradise at the Baptisterio, the Duomo, David, the Uffizi, and the Palazzo Pitti.

Naples, in the south, was the liveliest of all Italian cities. An excavating engineer broke a piece off the mosaic in Pompeii and presented it to me. (He serenaded me every night in front of the hotel window. In order not to become overwhelmed by so much passion I had to leave the city earlier than intended). I met Axel Munthe's turtle in the gardens of San Michele on Capri and waited for the green arrow to appear at sunset on Ischia. There were Palermo, Segesta, and Selinunte. I entered Demeter's sanctuary in Girgenti and stepped in the "Ear of Dionysius" in Syracuse.

Two other summers I went by car from Dieppe in France, to Spain, and crossed over to North Africa (Tangier and Tétouan). When I asked my English travel companion if the British had made peace with Joan of Arc, our car broke down, on cue, just in front of Orleans on Good Friday, and we were late for the Semana Santa in Seville.

Another car broke down in the middle of the Moroccan Rif Mountains on the way back from Chaouen to which the Muslims had fled after having been driven out of Cordoba. This event freed the money Ferdinand and Isabella gave Columbus to discover India (actually, America). I caught up with my fellow travelers, in a taxi with a harem's woman and a foreign legionnaire in handcuffs to be taken to his court martial.

Vivid in my memory are the caves of Altamira with bisons of another age. From there I visited the cathedral of Salamanca; the walled city of Avila, Ferdinand and Isabella's castle in Segovia, El Greco's house and the ruins of the civil war in Toledo. I experienced the Royal Crypt with the tombs of great emperors in the Escorial, the paintings in the Prado of Madrid, the gypsies' fandango at the Almacén outside of Granada, the Alhambra, The Great Mosque of Cordoba, and the bullfighter school at Valencia. At the empty beach at Benidorm we shared our wine with the coastal guard and kept the fire on an agave root going through the night. Mallorca raised memories of Chopin and we walked on La Rambla in Barcelona and drove to Montserrat Monastery high up in the coastal mountains.

Back in Berlin, I continued writing and organized readings with budding writers and actors, some of them became quite famous later on.

In 1955, when I was thirty-five years old, I went to the United States. My task in Europe was finished. My father received his retirement pay, so I could leave. I had met a girl in the Labor Service who, born in Texas, had come to Berlin in 1939, and was forced to stay when World War II broke out. After the war, I persuaded her to go back and help her ailing father in Houston, Texas. While she was nursing her father, she went to university and got a teaching degree. She kept writing that I should come, too.

But before I talk about my arrival in the United States, we have to look at my roots.

⚘ ⚘ ⚘

I have no doubt about my roots though they may not always be visible. We take our roots with us wherever we go. (Gertrude Stein took hers to France.)

On my father's side, I am one-eighth French. The Chapron were Huguenots who, in the 17th century, came from Metz to Berlin to escape persecution. The Prussian king, Frederick the Great, had offered asylum. One of my French ancestors co-founded the Charite, a large hospital in Berlin where famous physicians worked. The other roots on my father's side can be found in the Mark Brandenburg, the province surrounding Berlin. Some of my paternal ancestors were skippers, most of them were artisans.

My father had been trained as an electrical engineer and became head of a department in a Jewish factory. He lost his job when the persecution of Jews began;

however, after a few months, he was called back because he was needed. (I learned from other sources that he had invented a machine and was sent to Paris to supervise its demonstration.)

My father was a quiet man who never expressed his emotions. Once I climbed on his lap, but he gently pushed me off. I asked him why he never showed his love and he answered, "We don't show emotions in our family." However, he spoke with great affection about me to others. He spanked me only once, for something I had not done. This violent outburst of temper was surprising and we never talked about it later. We never talked much about anything anyway. We related mainly on non-verbal levels.

After work, all his attention went into a small garden he had rented at the outskirts of Berlin. He wanted to create a safe place for me to play. It took him over ten years to convert sand dunes at the banks of the river Spree into a blooming and fruit-bearing piece of land. Though the lot was small, there was an abundance of apple, pear, cherry and apricot trees; bushes with currant and gooseberries; strawberry patches; spinach and radishes; and flowers everywhere. He especially enjoyed pruning and cultivating roses. It was truly a "secret garden." The vegetables saved us from starvation during and after the war. My father rebuilt the small sunnier house which had burned down during the last days of the war. After his retirement, he became president of this group of city dwellers who wanted to stay in touch with nature. I share his love of nursing growth and connecting with nature.

❀ ❀ ❀

My mother was a stern and status-conscious woman. She was generous to everybody who visited us. Retrospectively, I think she must have been very lonely, and frigid, too. However, there were rare moments of communication, when we could read each other's thoughts. This kind of communication was natural for me and I thought everybody could do it. People kept wondering why I would answer a question which had not been heard and why, after some minutes of silence, my mother would respond to another unheard thought.

When I was an actress in Neustrelitz, north of Berlin, I once heard my mother's voice in the storm outside my window. I answered and the storm seemed to subside. I wrote the day and hour of this event into my diary and forgot about it. After two months, I visited my parents in Berlin and my mother went immediately to the calendar and asked me whether I had talked to her the day and the hour I had heard her voice several hundred miles away.

I like my West Prussian roots. My mother was born in a small village close to the (former) Polish border. The village now lies deep in Poland, where German enclaves have existed for centuries, especially around the city of Posen. Though intermarriages occurred, one could always distinguish the two ethnic groups by their religion. The Germans were Lutheran and the Polish were Catholic. My mother told me that during World War I, Catholic priests had preached from the pulpit that the farmers should take their sickles and "mow" down the heads of Germans.

When I visited the village in the thirties, no racial tension could be felt. It was rather a creative tension between people who value their own tradition and try to preserve it but have learned to respect other belief systems, simply because they have to live so closely together.

As far as I know, the melting pot theory never worked. We have to accept the fact that we live in multi-ethnic, multi-religious, and even multi-lingual communities. Sometimes, creative solutions may develop, sometimes different belief systems harden the differences and lead to tragic consequences. In 1993-1994, we witnessed, for example, the tragic multi-ethnic and multi-religious tensions in Bosnia where people for centuries have lived peacefully next to each other. At the time I am writing these lines, there is no end to the killing of neighbors by neighbors in sight.

I carried the knowledge of coexisting belief systems into my later work. Yes, people can peacefully coexist in the same geographic area. I founded, for example. Independent Scholars of Asia, Inc., to foster a better understanding between East and West with diametrically opposed world views.

My parents and I went many summers to West Prussia to help my maternal relatives with the harvest. I would stack the bundles of rye in the barn and milk the cows. I still smell the bread coming out of the brick oven, with small pieces of charcoal attached. Bread never tasted so good, especially with the butter I hand cranked out of the butter machine, by turning the handle for at least half an hour.

Once, I was entrusted with a herd of sheep and was horrified when they began to jump up and down and turn around in circles. Was this an epidemic? Did the sheep go crazy? I ran home in panic, and my aunt, my mother's sister, laughed heartily. She told me, "Get the sheep out of the clover, fast! You never should have allowed them to eat clover, it goes to their heads!" So I hastened back and stopped the bacchanal of my sheep. The way they looked at me, it was obvious that I was spoiling their fun.

I remember my uncle driving me in a horse-drawn carriage through the nearby woods. Early in the morning, the deer and the boars would tolerate the horse and would continue grazing or cross our way peacefully.

I remember the huge bush of lilac in front of the room where I slept. The thrushes would greet the sun in the morning and, at night, a big moon would hang in its branches. The air was full of fragrance mixed with some healthy smells from the stables. I still greet the sun every morning when it rises over the Berkeley hills.

Ghosts had been spotted in the room where I was sleeping and, impressionable as I was, I prepared myself for a possible encounter. The huge featherbed was my protection. I pulled the cool white linen over my head, trusting that no ghosts would slip under my cover. When I awoke, I saw a tall white shape standing in front of me. I froze. The ghost looked straight into my eyes. I could not run away; it was too close, it would follow me. So I went toward it and felt an icy cold slap on my forehead. I was petrified. It took me a couple of minutes to realize what actually had happened. The moon had lit the shape from behind so I could not recognize the face. But when I was fully awake, I saw myself standing in front of a large mirror. Sleepwalking, I had touched the frame with my feet and had partially woken up. When I went forward, my forehead hit the glass. I had spooked myself! And yes, I remembered my first round with ghosts when I had been a small child.

When one of my cousins married, the whole village was invited. We celebrated for eight days and eight nights. Two orchestras alternated and people danced to exhaustion. Several houses had been emptied and beds were ready for those who needed some rest. Friendly hands quickly changed the linen after guests had rested and returned to the celebration. Over a hundred chickens, several pigs and deer had been roasted. Rooms were filled with delicious, rich cakes, and there was a sack of coffee beans. It was believed that one could stabilize one's stomach by eating a handful of coffee beans. At my next visit, I asked my cousin when the wedding night had taken place and she confessed, "eight days later." They had slept for a whole week to catch up.

It was a large family who lived to the fullest. My mother had eighteen brothers and sisters, from three marriages. My grandfather had been married before he married my grandmother and my grandmother married again after he had prematurely died at the end of the last century. All eighteen uncles and aunts had numerous children too. In a rural family, as many hands as possible were needed to work in the fields.

When I was in my teens, I went through the village where my maternal grandfather had been administrator of a large princely estate and was surprised when a woman invited me into her house. She had never met me before but said I looked very much like my grandfather. (I had never seen him because he had died twenty-five years before I was born.) She wanted to show her gratitude for his kindness. He had saved several women from the princely right of the first night and had helped her to get started after her marriage. He also had been a healer. I was proud to be his grandchild.

The aunt from West Prussia would send us smoked ham or ducks for Christmas. In the city, food was not in abundance, but my mother still tried to excel herself when relatives came to celebrate birthdays. There were many birthdays in her family, almost one every week. More than thirty adults and dozens of children would mill around in our city apartment. Each celebration was preceded by days of cooking and baking. There were tubs with fried and pickled herring, huge roasts, cakes (each made with at least one pound of butter and twenty eggs which I had to beat and stir). Today, my stomach can no longer tolerate this kind of food, but good food and a good laugh are still important.

The war put an end to these feasts, which were never resumed. In 1945, East Germany and East Berlin were occupied by the Russian Army and our West Prussian relatives were put into Polish detention camps. Two small children were released and remembered our Berlin address. They stayed for a while with us, until their parents arrived and all went to Bavaria. Most of the family from my mother's side have died; the rest speak Bavarian because the girls (and there had only been girls on that side of the family) married Bavarian men and converted to Catholicism. I have visited them a couple of times and we send each other letters for birthdays and Christmas but we "don't speak the same language anymore."

I did not know my grandparents. Both grandparents on my mother's side and my paternal grandmother had died before I was born. I remember only the father of my father, a friendly looking man who glanced at me from across a table; but my mother stood between us and did not let him come closer. I never saw him again. He died when I was in my teens.

❀ ❀ ❀

I have remained the traveler who carries her roots with her and enjoys stepping into new territory. I need challenges to assert myself.

Once somebody told me, "You are like a deep well. When somebody throws a stone down the well and waits for an echo, he may be disappointed. However, when most of us have given up, the echo comes back so thunderous that it is frightening." It is true, my reactions seem to be delayed because it is important for me to process impressions first. I also hold back because people become frightened when I talk about the Source. I have learned to convey the message by living it.

Another friend told me that I take things too seriously, hide my feelings and over-control myself. I don't think so. In fact, I joke a lot. The role of a trickster and joker allows the freedom necessary to express ourselves without being taken too seriously. I don't like small talk but am ready to dance with and without people when the time is right.

When I am not working with people, I prefer silence. I need time to sort out all of my connections, renew myself and be nourished. The "inner space" needs protection from pollution. To recognize Infinite Love in its workings, we have to clear our "vision." When the close family does not offer sufficient encouragement, love and security, interconnections protect us from self-pity. Creative work provides the satisfaction we need.

As a young girl I painted a picture of a blue-clad woman carrying a bowl with a flaming heart. I envisioned offering myself in the service of others. This sounds rather corny. Some of my sacrifices appeared to be in vain. Most so-called "heroic" sacrifices, indeed, turn out to be ego trips, cravings for love and attention. The real sacrifice lies in blending into the landscape, not jumping out of it.

In 1955, paying for the passage myself, I took my roots to America. Being only twelve passengers on an American freighter, we were spoiled. We ate with the officers and had the run of the ship. Then, for three days and nights, the ship was rocked by a hurricane and I could not sleep. The crew called me the ship's ghost because I wandered around, fully clad. I was firmly resolved to die standing up.

On arrival in New York, my rain coat was stolen in the customs office while I interpreted for an elderly woman who did not speak English. The Berlitz School offered me $25 an hour for producing German language records but I did not want to stay in New York and went to see my friend in Illinois (she was the girl from Texas I have talked about before. She was now studying at Illinois State University). The university cities, Normal-Bloomington, were showcases of "gracious living." An American family prepared my first Thanksgiving dinner which made me feel at "home" and I was interviewed by the city editor for the local newspaper. After eight days, however, it was obvious that I would not get any other job than dishwasher. So I decided to go to Chicago.

Having paid the train ticket and one-week stay at the YWCA, I had less than ten dollars left. The first day I made the rounds of TV stations and was invited to talk "live" about East/West relations in Europe. They did not even offer me a cup of coffee. The second day I had to find work fast, so I went to the Department of Labor and was told the best I could expect would be an office job. I asked for addresses of publishing houses and the personnel manager of the first publishing house I went to — Wilcox & Follett, 1000 West Washington — told me they needed somebody for the German side of a German-English dictionary but did not have the money to pay me. I asked for addresses of special agencies and, by then, had to walk ten long blocks down Washington Street back to the Loop. When I arrived at the special agency, they were already waiting at the door and told me to go back to Wilcox & Follett where they had found the money to hire me. The next day I confessed that I had only a quarter left. The personnel manager did not believe me, but it turned out that she had to go on a promotional tour and needed a house sitter. She also gave me a personal loan of $100 which lasted until pay day. I was back in the middle of the stream, dancing.

I worked for one year as an editor in Chicago, drawing satisfaction out of exploring the different implications of German words translated into English, and English words translated into German. I also reviewed manuscripts of children's books for publication and took courses at the University of Chicago. On weekends, I explored the countryside of Illinois and Michigan, the woods in their fall coloring, Lincoln's grave in Springfield, and the huge Lake — soaking up the American landscape.

However, the humidity of one Chicago summer drained my energies. I quit my editor's job and went with a friend to San Francisco. While I was holding the "stone" in my hands, we drove down Route 66, with our household goods on top and two outdoor cats in the car. The cats hated the car, and could be heard howling, along with the ironing board at the bottom of our belongings on top of the car, during the whole trip. I saw Huckleberry Finn's country and the white picket fence in Hannibal.

The rich tapestry of the American landscape kept unfolding beginning with the red barns of Kansas. Then came the grandeur of the Rockies at Eagles Nest, Colorado. Traveling on to Taos with the Pueblo intact, but empty beer bottles in the cemetery, and then on to Santa Fe. In Arizona we saw the Painted Desert, the Petrified Forest, the Grand Canyon (I had never before seen sand and rock in so many colors, Sunset Crater, Meteor Crater, and the wide open space of the Mojave Desert. My American friend was frightened by the vast landscape, but I felt immensely relieved by this openness.

In San Francisco, I worked as technical translator for an international company. Our engineers built dams in Brazil and Pakistan and worked on the tunnel under the English Channel. They were wonderful musicians in their spare time. One of them designed the logo for my theater company, but I don't want to get too much ahead of myself.

I bought a monthly Greyhound bus ticket and whenever I was entitled to a vacation, I explored the United States, going from the Carlsbad Caverns to the Florida Keys. I visited the battlefields at Gettysburg and watched th e Amish living in a time warp in Pennsylvania. I took the "stone" and chanted with Native American Indians at their pow wows. A German painter, the holder of the Bear Knife, introduced me to the Blackfoot Indians in Wyoming, and I began to collect Native American tales about the origin of the world and how to stay in balance with the universe. In northern California, I was allowed to watch the Hupa White Deer Skin Dance, a ritual of world renewal that is still performed every year on the Hupa Reservation. (Do we Westerners have any ritual to restore the balance of our community? Are football or baseball games the only means to offer cathartic release?).

I took my stone to Hawaii and swam on Christmas Eve in the Pacific Ocean. I went to Mexico and Guatemala where I climbed the overgrown steps of the pyramids at Tikal, pulling myself up on branches or sliding on lose stones, all the time watching out for snakes and scorpions. Despite being covered from head to toe, I was terribly stung by mosquitoes. During the years since then, the pyramids have been excavated and visitors now miss much of the drama.

In 1960, I went around the world to explore Asia, a trip which had been unthinkable twenty years earlier. I needed the confirmation of being alive. I needed to meet new challenges by traveling to Japan, Hong Kong, Thailand, Cambodia (Angkor Wat before it became a war zone), Singapore, Sri Lanka, and India.

Visiting the Shah's treasure in Tehran (Iran) triggered my aversion to accumulations of wealth. The beauty of the precious stones had no other function than to demonstrate power. I was, however, nourished when I walked through the ruins of Persepolis (Iran) and paid my respect at the graves of Sufi poets.

I am grateful that I could see Beirut (Lebanon) before it was destroyed and will never forget the camel I rode at Baalbek. Young and fiery, it took off with me into the desert. We had to be rounded up by a posse. Asking why it had taken so long to "catch" us, the guides said they had been laughing so hard. While the camel had disappeared with me in a cloud of dust, I could be heard shouting, "Where are the brakes? Where are the brakes?" Experiencing a camel in its prime had been worth the risk. It was not trotting wearily along, swaying from side to side; it had run with the speed of an arrow. The thought of falling off did not even occur to me.

❦ ❦ ❦

Back in the United States, I founded a German-American theater group — the Art Repertory Theater. Some of my players were professional actors, some I trained over the years. We played comedies and tragedies at San Francisco and Santa Clara State Universities, Monterey Language Institute, University of California, Berkeley, and the City Club, in San Francisco. We played in German but our audiences were not only German immigrants; many Americans came and supported our efforts to bridge cultures.

Twice a month, I invited professionals to literary readings in my apartment and the idea of the "Universal Dialogue" took shape. Speakers from many disciplines donated their time to discuss topics of concern. I offered a safe space for the informal exchange of thoughts, feelings, aspirations and plans. All could speak freely and were stimulated and encouraged in their own work.

I was now sure that I wanted to continue working in America and decided to become a U.S. citizen in 1962.

When my office job began to absorb too much time and my vocation did not pay my rent, I volunteered for the Peace Corps and asked to be sent to Thailand, a country I had visited in 1960. Living in Asia for one year, I wanted to explore the different world views in more depth. I wanted, also, to finally embark on a university career to "legitimize" my work.

At that time, volunteers for Thailand were trained at the University of Washington in Seattle. With Mt. Rainier towering over the campus, the symbiosis of nature, body, emotions, mind, spirit and soul was invigorating. I remember sloshing through ice and snow from one lecture hall to another. At night, we sat in the language lab and transcribed, for example, the story of *Little Red Riding Hood* in Thai back into English from tapes made by our Thai teachers.

✿ ✿ ✿

In February 1963, my father in Berlin, took seriously ill. While the others departed for Thailand, I went back to the city where I was born, to nurse my father. The first three months I stayed the whole day with him in the hospital. In November, he had another stroke. This time, we kept him at home. He died two years later, on February 3, 1965.

I also took care of my mother who told me that, "Children think only of themselves," but I knew my priorities and, each night, warmed her bed with my body.

At night, when my parents were safely asleep, I taught adult education courses: Anthropology, English, and French. Assuming I needed Latin for my university career, I took lessons and passed the Great Latinum. Finally, after a special entrance exam, I began to study Anthropology, Sanskrit, and Southeast Asian cultures at the Free University of Berlin.

During the five summers in Germany, I found someone to take care of my parents and went to explore the Greek islands. I was literally looking for Ithaca, in the country of Homer. As a woman I could not enter Mount Athos but I took my "stone" to the Meteora monasteries high up on the Thessalonian mountains to which the monks had fled centuries ago. We drove up in a minibus where the monks earlier had to be pulled up in baskets. In one of the monasteries, a large wall painting of the Last Judgment depicted the three worlds (heaven-earth-hell). It was the same concept of the Three Worlds I had found in Thai wall paintings in 1960 and would study more intensively ten years later.

In the morning, I would stroll to the harbor of Piraeus and select island cruises, e.g., to Mykonos and Apollo's island of Delos, to the mysterious temples of Samothrake, to the extinguished volcano of Thera, to Patmos (the cave where St. John "en-visioned" the apocalypse).

I talked with a peasant woman on Euboea while we both enjoyed the hot springs. Though I could not understand her Greek and she did not understand my classic Greek either, something was conveyed. We spoke the universal language of the heart. Later, somebody wrote letters for her in French and we corresponded for quite some time, verbally and non-verbally.

I remember the sound and light show at the Parthenon when the runner from Marathon arrived to announce the defeat of the Persians. We could hear his footsteps and his shout of "victory," "victoire," "Sieg," whatever language group was listening. His last gasp had a rather comical effect.

I roamed the bazaar of Istanbul, walked through the different Troys in Asia Minor and stood in the amphitheater of Ephesus, which seemed to echo the voice of St. Paul. I found the house where Mary spent her last years, but there was hardly any trace of the Temple of the Hundred-Breasted Artemis. (Herostratos had burned the temple to get into the history books. How many Herostratos live among us now?) Not much was left of the Mausoleum of Halicarnassus, one of the Seven Wonders of the World, but its spirit was still alive, despite encrustations of later "civilizations" brought in by crusaders and Turks.

I spent two summers on Crete, soaking up the Minoan culture at Cnossos and Paestos, climbing into the cave of the Cretan Zeus on the hill which overlooks the plain, with the wind mills of Lasithi. I swam in the Mediterranean at sunrise. The waters that had carried so many cultures from continent to continent embraced my body.

I remember the fruits of the sea, the fresh crabs and lobsters, put directly on the charcoal grill. At dusk, the sea became violet blue, as Homer had said, with the sun sprinkling golden sparks on the velvety waves. The Greek landscape was very healing and my 'stone' kept absorbing new cultures.

❧ ❧ ❧

My mother died on December 12, 1967. I partially sold, but mostly gave away, what had been left of my German past and kept only my books and manuscripts. The sale of my piano paid for my first tuition at the University of California, Berkeley.

❦ ❦ ❦

On my return to the San Francisco Bay Area in fall of 1968, I excavated my belongings from a friend's basement in Daly City, and moved to Berkeley. The books were slightly damaged by an unforeseen flood and, in my absence, too many feet had stepped on my bear rug (a survivor of my "Medea" performance in San Francisco ten years before). The pile of my worldly goods and I were finally reunited and I was ready for the next step.

Now, at 48, I began to study for my B.A. in Anthropology at the University of California, Berkeley, financing my studies by working fifteen hours each week at the university, with professors of my Anthropology department. During the first quarter, I also took five courses and excavated an Indian mound on weekends. I was insatiable.

I had not been given credit for anything I had done before, so I took one exam after the other, getting credit for my Great Latinum, my drama studies, the interpreter certificates (English, German, Italian, Spanish, and French). After one year, it turned out I had more credits than necessary and the B.A. was awarded in the middle of the student revolution. I found myself walking through clouds of pepper and tear gas on campus. Once I went crying to an opera performance in San Francisco, because a police car had emptied their tank into my face while I was walking down the street with an armful of books. (Incidentally, somebody forgot to invite me to my graduation ceremony.)

My visions and my intent, the resolve of my inner experiences, however, carried me safely through the vicissitude of political, social, and scholarly turmoil.

It took two years to write my M.A. thesis on a social-cultural comparison of a Thai custom for which I had not only done library research but also interviewed Thai students in the Bay Area and added memories of my earlier visit to Thailand in 1960.

All my professors were younger than I, but anticipating possible difficulties in communication, I had taken a vow of silence. This was easy because I had learned to keep a straight face as an actress.

The story of my master's thesis gives some taste of the scene. When I told the chairman of my thesis committee, who had avoided me for a whole year, that he would have to read my thesis because I was going to submit it within two days, he answered that I should look for another chairman. He knew that, being fifty, I did not want to lose more time, so he obviously expected me to grovel. I waited until he had left the room and phoned another professor, asking him whether he could read my thesis overnight. Then I ran to the Graduate Division and changed my committee. I was back within one hour. The professor appeared again and told me that I should look for another chairman. I silently showed him the paper which proved I had done exactly what he had told me to do. He exploded. My interconnectedness had given me the strength to stay calm.

❦ ❦ ❦

During my second stay in Asia, 1971-1972, I conducted fieldwork in Thailand to collect data for my dissertation on the role of Buddhism in an Asian country. I had selected Thailand because it had never been colonized and Buddhism had been the state religion for at least seven hundred years.

Nobody would give a fifty-year-old woman a grant, so I financed the field work with my savings. I also taught English for half a year at the University of Chiang Mai in northern Thailand.

During my studies at the University of California, Berkeley, I had already compared the mindfulness of breathing with the Indian concept of "prana" and the Malay concept of "angin" (wind). Now I spent much of my time in Buddhist monasteries and began to meditate regularly, practicing what I had learned from books. I still remember the abbot of a meditation monastery in northern Thailand laughing heartily when I described my unsuccessful attempts in meditation. He said one word, "Sit!" All of a sudden, I understood that, despite my scriptural knowledge, I had not included body aware-ness. The results — and benefits — were surprising and I progressed with ease.

During the year in Southeast Asia, I also visited Burma with a group of women from the National Museum in Bangkok. I had volunteered to work on the Srivijaya room. When we landed in Rangoon, no other plane was on the ground and machine guns were pointed at us from surrounding airport buildings. In the hotel elevator, we met Russian delegates, from whom our guide had tried to keep us, but we managed to live through the political taboos. We became engrossed in the splendor of The Great Stupa at Rangoon. A special plane took us during the eight days allotted to the old capital of Mandalay where the palace, considered to be the center of the country, was still surrounded by a moat. The Bud-dhist Canon, inscribed on marble slabs, could be read in the galleries leading to a monastery on the Sagaing Hills. We saw Pagan, the city of hundreds of stupas, before many of them crumbled during an earthquake. In the Shan states, we floated to the villages on stilts in the Inle Lake. What impressed us most was the inner beauty of the Burmese who continue their simple life with dignity, secure in their Buddhist practices.

I drove with several hundred of my students from the University of Chiang Mai to a sport event in northeast Thailand. When we crossed the Mekong into Laos, I landed in a police station and had to be bailed out by my own students. We had forgotten that I needed a visa, even for the one-day excursion.

To compare my field data with other Buddhist groups, I went also on field trip where I talked to Tibetan lamas outside of Kathmandu (Nepal) and visited Buddhist enclaves on Java. I walked the pilgrim's path through the galleries of the World of Desire, the World of Form and the World of No-Form of the Borobodur. The monasteries on Sri Lanka were still active and blended well with the monuments of a great Buddhist past at Anuradhapura and Polonnaruwa. Frictions became visible between the Sinhalese (who were mostly Buddhists) and the Tamil (who were mostly Hindu), though I heard that Buddhists and Hindu alike would fire walk once a year at Kataragama.

Shortly before submittal, I was not satisfied with my dissertation and rewrote it in two days and two nights. The Ph.D. in Asian Studies was awarded by the University of California, Berkeley. In 1974 and I began to teach Indian Religions at Mills College in Oakland. In contrast to my predecessor, who had three students, I found that eighteen students had enrolled in my course and each of them wrote a research paper. The course was, however, discontinued for more marketable skills—book keeping.

I finally had to face the fact that a woman over fifty has passed her chance for a tenure position. Never accepting any "reality" as final, I founded Independent Scholars of Asia, a non-profit, professional, self-help organization which teaches other scholars to continue their professional work without the backing of a university.

In 1975, I received a post-doctoral travel grant to India. At that time, I also visited Taiwan, Thailand, Sri Lanka, and Germany, to set up research projects.

❦ ❦ ❦

In the United States, I continued my meditation practices and became president of a meditation group in the San Francisco Bay Area. I taught meditation myself, and edited a series of transcribed lectures by my Burmese meditation master.

I later edited, *The Four Foundations of Mindfulness*, a book dedicated to the memory of my parents. After ten years of Buddhist activities, however, I had to withdraw from the Buddhist Council of Northern California because infighting deflected too much energy away from other important work. I had to stay available for urgent needs which had made themselves known.

We have to watch where we are going. Outside influences and daily tasks can put layers on the Inner Source and cloud our visions. We should be warned not to underestimate this process, which is aggravated by inertia.

I remember that once I felt depressed for an unusually long time, "My well had run dry."

At times we are confronted with the great terror of complete darkness—physical, emotional, mental, social, and spiritual nothingness. Horridas nostrae mentis purga tenebras! (Purge the horrible darknesses of our mind!). *The Aurora Consurgens*, an alchemical treatise ascribed to Thomas Aquinas, speaks of the "horrible darkness of our mind" and the necessity of cleansing ourselves from this terror—complete darkness, no light, no sound, no touch, no smell, no taste; neither form nor any sign of life. This darkness stuns our senses, stupefies our reasoning, and immobilizes us to the point of becoming unable to think or act. Suffering appears to be infinite and we feel helpless. Escape appears to be impossible!

So I decided to go on a "journey." Recalling the effectiveness of sound, I asked somebody to drum for me for ten minutes.

I found myself walking toward this "horrible darkness." Was I about to die? Darkness was ahead of me—infinite darkness. I knew I had to walk into this darkness where nothing could be found. I felt if I would continue to walk I would be dissolved into nothing. There was no escape. I was convinced I was about to die. My fate appeared to be irreversible. The hopelessness was overwhelming and the pain unbearable.

But then I realized that a brilliant light was touching my shoulders and the back of my head. Infinite Light was behind me. I was in the light. And there were others. We all were carrying the light into the darkness.

The vision had started with complete despair and ended on an ecstatic note. Nothing did actually change but my consciousness. It shifted. What is more natural than looking into darkness, when we are in the light? When we see the light in front of us, then we are in the darkness!

This moment of clear perception made me aware of the "brainwashing" we undergo during the so-called acculturation processes at home, at school, and during our professional career. I had allowed the memory that we are in the light to fade. That's what Adam and Eve forgot when they were driven out of the Garden of Eden. They allowed a guilt complex to obscure the true nature of their being.

Through a shift in consciousness I got a glimpse of what shamans and mystics experience. They learn to tap this energy and offer themselves to become channels through which divine messages can descend. To carry the light into the darkness becomes a life-long commitment which we hesitate to talk about because it can easily be misunderstood. The commitment entails a continuous process of learning. Each day we have to penetrate the manifold manifestations of darkness surrounding us.

To balance and replenish myself, I could access the Source by listening to music, by dancing, swimming and meditating. However, I also needed to develop further skills.

I learned to breathe from the diaphragm during my training as an actress and during my meditation practices. Out-breathing allows release of mental blocks as well as physical tension, and in-breathing nourishes and replenishes energy.

I also learned to create an invisible shield around me with my breath. This shield not only protects me when I feel vulnerable, it also signals when danger comes too close. It serves as a "radar screen." For example, when the Russians conquered Berlin in April 1945 and searched all buildings to plunder and rape, my shield went up and the Russian soldiers, for no apparent reason, went past the place I was hiding. They "did not see me." Of course, I did not really "disappear," it was my shield that distracted their attention. Some decades later, I sensed an oncoming assault on the streets of San Francisco and thwarted the attempt by turning around in time and "shifting the attention" of the attacker. Such "shift" is possible only from a place of "complete relaxation and interconnectedness."

Over the years, I developed further non-verbal means to raise the life force. I cultivated, for example, the use of my hands (Reiki I and II). Holding them approximately one inch away from a client's body, I started with the head and moved my hands slowly down the body, allowing the energy to rise. I was not consciously "doing" anything. I waited for the energy to rise naturally and then connected the other to the Source.

❦ ❦ ❦

In 1978, I was awarded a Fulbright-Hays Research Grant to study shamans and mediums. For one year, I was stationed at the Institute of Southeast Asia Studies in Singapore. I traveled repeatedly to Thailand, Malaysia, Indonesia, the Philippines, Sumatra, Sabah, and Sarawak. I fully appreciated and used this opportunity to absorb more aspects of Asian cultures.

❦ ❦ ❦

The stone was with me when a remarkable shamaness outside Bangkok healed for three days and three nights without getting up from her seat. The stone was with me when a tribal shamaness in northern Thailand rode into the spirit world. Sitting on a bench, blindfolded, she bobbed up and down as if riding on a horse. Once in a while she would jump up to greet a spirit and ask for the whereabouts of the lost soul she tried to retrieve. In Southern Thailand, I inquired whether a legend was true. I had heard that shamans become tigers after death. A simple fisherman answered, "Do you want to see it?" and, after one hour of evocations, he behaved like a tiger, making giant leaps from one wall to the other. In Singapore, a simple dock worker transformed into the God Rama. I sat with his community around the snake altar while he conveyed messages from a different realm, his eyes glowing with divine fire.

Attending the Tenth International Congress of Anthropological and Ethnological Sciences in New Delhi (India), I was invited to explore Orissa [aka Odisha] as guest of state. I enjoyed this status and had a limousine at my disposal. I set up a research project to study tribal cultures in the following stages of acculturation:

1. still upholding the traditional ways,
2. in the process of acculturating to the mainstream Indian culture
3. fully acculturated

I returned frequently to Asia to explore the wide range of trances with my shaman friends. This knowledge is shared in my "Universal Dialogue" series, my conferences, and my work with clients.

My hunger for more knowledge and my intent to share what I learned, led to accepting invitations to lecture on several different cruises. In January 1983, I went to Asia. From January to May 1985, I went with twenty students of the International School, through India: New Delhi, Agra, Vrindaban, and Benares. We continued into Nepal: Kathmandu and Pokkara (riding an elephant at dawn). Then we traveled to Thailand (studying life in Bangkok, Chiang Mai, and other tribes). We continued on to Hong Kong and then to mainland China, visiting Yunnan (where the White Mountain Tiger and the Blue Dragon meet at Kunming Lake). We concluded our journey in Japan, visiting Kyoto and Nara (exploring most of the over four hundred Buddhist monasteries and Shinto temples).

My students took America with them wherever they went. They behaved like proverbial horses whom we lead to water and then have to wait until they are ready to drink. It is almost impossible to measure the influence teachers have on their students. I have given up measuring my effectiveness as a teacher. I am satisfied with having remained honest, knowing I have given without holding back. Once, after ten years, a student wrote to me that I had changed his life. It was rather late in coming, but I appreciated the fact that he still felt the need to let me know how I had affected him.

In 1986, I went on a friendship tour through Helsinki to Russia. I had always felt close to the Russian mentality, attracted by its mixture of healthy strength and sensitivity. The first step on Russian soil, and especially the visit to the cemetery of Leningrad, brought back war memories — the immense suffering of people on "both sides." I cried for the Russians as I had cried for the millions of dead Germans. The city of Leningrad, now St. Petersburg, reminded me of Prussian architecture in

Potsdam. The Spirit of reshaping a country manifested independently in very similar form in Germany and in Russia.

I felt as though I were walking through the calm before a storm, not only when walking through the catacombs of Kiev (Ukraine), but also in the city. Two weeks later this uneasy feeling was made manifest in the incident at Chernobyl.

In Soci, a shaky helicopter carried me over the Caucasus. I swam, in the middle of winter, in the heated open-air pool of the hotel, which held water from the Black Sea.

In May 1987, I lectured on a Pearl Cruise from Kobe to Nagasaki, Dalian, Beijing, Yantai, Tsingdao, Shanghai, Suzhou, Wuxi, Xiamen, and Hong Kong. The effects of the first atom bombs, dropped on Hiroshima and Nagasaki, will remain imprinted on all our minds.

Again I entered a communist country and sensed the restraints on the Chinese soul. There were not many cars on the streets, but thousands of Chinese sleep-bicycled in front of speeding trucks (and they don't even believe in reincarnation or nirvana).

While I walked on The Great Wall, time did not stand still because thousands of Chinese walked with me. It was, literally, wall to wall people. (Mao had asked the Chinese to walk on the wall at least once in their lifetime).

The Forbidden City of Beijing was no longer secret. Everybody could admire the Palace Museum which was full of incredible art treasures. I laughed about the marble boat of the Empress Dowager who spent the money collected for creating the Chinese navy on a boat which never will sail. Maybe if we all donated money to build some marble 'star wars' in the White House garden, it would stop war instantly.

The white beaches of Tsingdao were filled with foreigners who were offered the opportunity to buy condominiums. I found rest only in front of the Jade Buddha in Shanghai. I savored the splendid "trading post" of Hong Kong, especially the tidbits in my old dim sum restaurant on Nathan Road.

In July 1988, I went to Czechoslovakia, Hungary, and Yugoslavia to explore other Eastern European countries. Prague had not been liberated yet, and the faces of the people on the street were empty, disconnected from the beauty of the castles and bridges. The Jewish cemetery evoked memories of Kafka and the Golem. And I attempted to tune into the large collections of early goddesses in the museum of Brno.

Budapest's spirit appeared to be indestructible and life affirming, as was a mime performance in the historical quarters on the hill. I enjoyed an invigorating swim in the thermal pools on Marguerite Island. I attended the XIIth International Congress of Anthropological and Ethnological Sciences in Zagreb. I met the visionaries in Medjugorje, to whom the Madonna still appears each day. Priests publish daily bulletins and "Her words" are posted outside the church where the crowd of pilgrims line up for confession. I walked through historical Mostar which has since been destroyed during the Bosnian war (the destruction of the old bridge was shown on TV). And I absorbed Dubrovnik.

❀ ❀ ❀

From May to June 1989, I went across Asia along the Silk Road, the same route which had been traveled for thousands of years by Indian monks who, accompanying merchants, brought Buddhism to China. I started on the other end, in Hong Kong, from where we flew to Shanghai. People were crowding the streets, hope on their faces. Nobody anticipated the massacre on Tiananmen Square two weeks later. We went inland to the old capital Xian, where the large underground army (cast in terracotta) is rising from the dust. We passed through Lanzhou and found, outside of Xining, the Tibetan monastery of Taer. Despite the Cultural Revolution, high lamas are still being consulted and prayer wheels have not stopped turning for centuries. There was the pagoda of Famen and its museum with Buddhist paraphernalia made of gold and precious jewels. Monks beckoned us to come into the crypt where they opened a small reliquary and showed us a finger bone of the Buddha. We entered a realm beyond time upon seeing the relic of a great teacher who had died over 2,500 years ago.

We went through Ledu and crossed the Gobi Desert, passing by nomads who still use the road with their camels carrying all their belongings. We needed special permission to enter some of Dunhuang's hundreds of caves where the walls are covered with religious paintings of different periods. We rode camels to the sand dunes and, in Turfan, walked through another cave city. Then we entered Muslim country and drove through Urumqi and Kashgar to Lake Karakol. We were supposed to sleep in one of the yurts but the news of the massacre on Tienanmen Square caught up with us and we had to leave China via the Karakoram on dangerous but incredibly beautiful mountain roads. Right and left on the rocks were petroglyphs of earlier pilgrims. Alongside the Indus River, our minibus finally found its way to the plain of Islamabad (Pakistan).

In October 1989 and February 1990, I lectured again on Pearl Cruises to Singapore, Phuket, Kuala Lumpur, Malacca, and Bangkok. In Spring 1991, I lectured on a C unard Cruise Line from Bombay, to Goa, the Moluccas, and some Malaysian islands, on a "diet" of champagne and caviar.

In July 1991, I participated in the Conference on Humanistic Psychology in Moscow, where Russian colleagues turned out to be more sophisticated in debate than their American colleagues. Very clear in their views, they had not yet been confused by the different kinds of psychology of the West. "Holotropic breathing" and shamanic workshops, however, have in the meantime reached Moscow together with McDonald's and Colonel Sander's Kentucky Fried Chicken.

In 1991, I was invited to speak at a conference on women in parapsychology in Dublin. Ireland is, indeed, a world by itself. I experienced Irish pride in its purest form during the reenactment of government procedures in City Hall. I followed James Joyce through Dublin and drank Guinness at its source. I drove along the coast of the green island where Vikings had landed and I stepped back thousands of years in the mound of Newgrange.

In January 1992, I went on a mystery journey to Egypt with Jean Houston where I stood in front of the oldest pyramid at Sakkara. The others were riding camels or roaming through the nearby ruins. For a few minutes I was alone, completely in awe. The pyramid had begun to vibrate. It pulsed in the bright sun light. When I raised my video camera, the light meter ceased to function and the strong white light filled me. Bright light was all around me. There it was again, "the Light." It claimed me, held me in its arms, and gave me new strength, as if it was giving me a new body. At the same time, I could hear and feel a strong wind. Everything was one, in the pulsating powerful light. The word "power" does not match this experience. It was Certainty. It was everything—a higher reality—the flow of creation.

Somebody called me to join the others. It was difficult to step back into consensus reality. I felt like the phoenix that had been burned to ashes and had risen again from the fire. I cherished the "new" strength, but knew, if communicated directly, the light would burn "unprepared matter." The strength had to be filtered to whatever I was doing in daily life.

I had this experience when I was 72 years old. At the time I am writing this book, I am 74, and should now say something about "age." When I became 50, I went into a deep depression. Half my life was over and I had not ach ieved what I wanted. I just had gotten my M.A. and was in the middle of a painful initiation process—working for my Ph.D. at a leading university. It was painful not so much because my knowledge was challenged; my stamina, my whole being was tested to its limits, and Berkeley was in the middle of the student revolution.

My childhood spirit, however, sent me rebellious dreams and so I sat down and devised a program which would keep the aging process "in check": diet, exercise, and mental hygiene. I continued swimming 40 minutes every day in the outdoor pool of the University of California, Berkeley. I established, every morning, a priority list of the many projects I am involved in, working in the order of their urgency. I have a tendency to get involved in more projects than I humanly can carry out, so things can easily become complicated without a daily changing priority list.

With increased awareness for the needs of the moment and the knowledge of 74 years how to react to demands, the mental hygiene part—spirit and soul—takes care of itself. I have kept my body in fairly good shape with the right diet and swimming. There are minor bouts of arthritis and lower back pains and the sight of my left eye is diminishing. The unavoidable deterioration of my body is balanced by the inner light shining through. Age really should not bother us too much. In fact, I enjoy my age because I am able to think clearer and more to the point. I act faster, with less hesitation; and look at any problem pragmatically, as well as idealistically, to come up with a balanced view, supporting interconnection. But let's get back to Egypt, 1992.

Our group went down the Nile, from the Aswan Dam to Cairo, first in a large houseboat and then by bus. Like Isis and Osiris, a couple was married in Osiris' temple of Abydos. I had participated in two of Jean's weekend events before and was grateful for her evocation of the spirit of Egypt's past. During an early morning ritual on the last day in the King's Chamber of the Great Pyramid at Giza, a crystal hit my third eye when I was lying in the sarcophagus. I returned from Egypt full of light.

۞ ۞ ۞

In July 1992, I participated in the Second Conference on Humanistic Psychology in Moscow, and also conducted workshops in Siberia (Novosibirsk). The beauty of the open spaces in Siberia and the lush vegetation of the taiga allowed the soul to grow.

Insatiable in my thirst for further explorations, I went in August 1992, to Yucatán (Mérida, Uxmal, Chichen Itza, Cobá, Tulum, Cancun); Villahermosa (Olmec); Oaxaca (Mt. Alban and Mitla); Mexico City, and Tula. It was my third visit to Mexico but this time I went with a small group and we took time to allow rituals to emerge.

In May, 1993, I fulfilled a long-standing wish and went to the Four Corners area of the U.S. — Mesa Verde, Monument Valley, Canyon de Chelly — rafting wild water on the San Juan River and sleeping under the stars. The strong presence and beauty of nature charges, like a giant battery, all who have kept their doors of perception open.

۞ ۞ ۞

In July 1993, I went again to Europe to look after the graves of my parents in Berlin. My premonitions turned out to be right. The cemetery authorities had done a bad job in care taking and planting flowers, so I had to take a spade myself. I weeded out grass and rearranged flowers and bushes.

The International Society for Shamanic Research (ISSR) which had been founded in 1989 in Zagreb (Yugoslavia), meets bi-annually. During the first meeting in Seoul (Korea), 1991, we watched Korean shamans climb sword ladders. One shaman channeled MacArthur. The Second ISSR Conference was held in Budapest in 1993. The large group of Russian scholars from Yakut brought new information and it was encouraging to see American, French, German, Italian, and Russian researchers discussing collaborative projects.

Afterwards I flew to the Baltic Sea where I conducted workshops in Vilnius (Lithuania) and at a sea resort outside of Tallinn (Estonia).

Returning for two days to the United States, I departed again for the XIIIth International Congress of Anthropological and Ethnological Sciences in Mexico City. It is always a joy to meet colleagues and friends after so many years. One day, I listened to South– and Meso-American instruments (turtle shells, clay pots, coconuts, etc.) in the Museum of Anthropology.

In the beginning of 1995, I went to Australia (Sidney and Cairns) exploring the Great Barrier Reef in a submarine. In the rain forest of Kurunda, on top of a mountain range, aborigines danced in a Hollywood like setting and bungee jumpers demonstrated their fearlessness.

On the North Island of New Zealand, I enjoyed sailing. I was surprised to see all the extinct volcanoes which

surround Auckland. In Rotorua, with geysers everywhere, the hotel was built in the caldera of a volcano. I
swam in its sulfur pool. We watched California trout thriv-
ing in the different climate and saw sheep dogs herding
their flock. The sheep were shorn in Hollywood style.
Even the elusive kiwi bird peaked out from bushes in
a dark room. The Māori performance in the hotel was
less impressive. Polynesian aggressiveness was filtered
through Christianity. They obliged tourists by using guitars.

The lake of Queenstown on the South Island appeared
to be breathing. There was Milford Sound, Mt. Cook Gla-
cier, and Christchurch in the Canterbury Plain. Here
a New Zealand couple invited us for a gourmet dinner.

Australian cities were very British. Aborigines were
not publicly talked about. On New Zealand, I could
walk briefly through a Māori village inside a geyser area
where the local Māori tolerated the tourists. It appeared
that they did not expect to be treated on an equal basis.
Ethnic barriers are hard to wear down.

❦ ❦ ❦

Since 1984, I have called over one hundred scholars and practitioners of shamanism, artists, philosophers,
and psychologists to participate, each year, in the International Conference on the Study of Shamanism
and Alternate Modes of Healing at the Santa Sabina
Center, in San Rafael, California, on Labor Day weekend. Opinions about shamanism and alternate modes
of healing vary and some practitioners' claims are mis-
leading. We decided to restore the dignity of a grossly
misrepresented profession which has served humanity
selflessly since time immemorial. We encourage and
stimulate each other. We participate in experiential
sessions and listen to healing music. Fourteen volumes

of proceedings have so far been published. They also include the transcribed discussions.

The term "shaman" is derived from a Tungus word. Siberian shamans became the prototype for Western scholars at the beginning of the century. Mircea Eliade, an historian of religion, collected secondary reports on shamans from all over the world and legitimized the study of shamanism which is now a concern of anthropologists, sociologists, folklorists, scholars of ethnomedicine and psychologists.

Shamans access different states of consciousness at will. They fulfill the needs of their community that otherwise are not met and are the true mediators between the Sacred and the Secular.

Some people say, "We are no longer willing to have a mediator between ourselves and the Divine." They don't know what they are talking about. Shamans have never prevented anyone from contacting the Divine, on the contrary, they facilitate the connection. Shamans work wherever they are invited to help. They don't advertise but can be found in times of need. Track records of shamans solving problems are available from respectable scholars.

Problematic are neo-shamans who make irresponsible claims. There is no reason to do anything about them. We don't need a licensing board for shamans. The law of natural selection takes care of impostors. That means people go to shamans who have a good success rate and naturally stay away from those who are unsuccessful.

To illustrate the kind of casualties shamanic and soul retrieval workshops may produce, I offer one case which speaks for itself:

After having taken a soul-retrieval workshop, a young woman performed a ritual to guide the soul of her brother (who had committed suicide) into the other world. When she listened to the tape recording she had made of the ritual, she found that she had taken the soul of her brother into her own body. Shortly after, she also incorporated the soul of a man she had briefly met and who had died suddenly of a heart attack. She was very confused and asked me to exorcise the two souls from her body. I proved to her that it is not so easy to incorporate somebody else's soul. We had to look at what her agitated mind and her fears had manifested. She was quite relieved and responded to the purification.

The next case exemplifies shamanic work: A middle-aged woman with migraine headaches had consulted physicians and psychotherapists for years but everything had failed. The migraine worsened to the point that she could no longer work professionally. I suspected psychological causes but did not encourage her to talk about her ailment, so that the "dis-ease" pattern would not be reinforced. I showed her some breathing exercises to release physical and emotional tension and gave her a full-body Reiki. She felt some release during the breathing and was surprised about the energy the Reiki treatment brought to the surface. She promised to do the breathing exercises daily and came back after a week. Being a desperate but intelligent woman, she had done well with the breathing and she said herself, she felt something had started to move. We did not talk much and again I gave her a full-body Reiki. The next morning she called to tell me that she was "purging," literally-she was vomiting, had diarrhea, and a childhood trauma had come up. Now she could openly deal with her problem. I had "shifted her attention" from the disease pattern to a point where change appeared to be possible. I had proven change to her when I raised her energy level, and I had shown her how to purge herself so that she could take over and interconnect on her own.

❧ ❧ ❧

With friends in Europe, Asia, Australia, New Zealand, and the United States, "home" is wherever I am. Fulfilling the needs of the moment, I continue to taste the sweetness and the bitterness of life.

We have to break through our isolation, mend our fragmented self-image and allow the creative power of Being to rise to the surface. We can be both "individuated and in harmonious balance with others and the environment" (Kryder, 1993:1). We can move and we can dance.

Each experience strengthens and reconfirms our mission. Each morning, the rising sun reminds us of our responsibility to transform negativities wherever they arise. It is our task to carry the light into the darkness. We need to carry it to those who suffer, to the many who are searching for meaning, to all who want to learn how to "connect."

So many people separate themselves from their body, feelings, mind, and soul. Alienated from themselves, they feel alienated also from others, from their society, their environment, and the universe. However, we all can dance in the middle of the stream and be nourished by the Source. We all can show the light to each other.

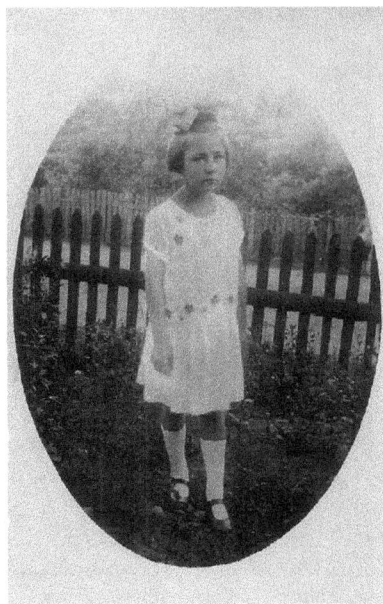

Ruth-Inge as a young girl

Ruth-Inge as a young woman

Portrait of Ruth-Inge as a young woman

Portrait of Ruth-Inge

Ruth-Inge in Kaiser Bad

Ruth-Inge drumming, 1999

Question and Answer, Group Discussion, Santa Sabina, Shamanism and Alternative Modes of Healing Conference, 1979

In 2006 Ruth-Inge was awarded the Honorary Medal of the 800th Anniversary of the Great Mongolian State by decree of the President of Mongolia for her contributions to understanding and promoting Mongolian culture.

Lucy Lewis dancing at Santa Sabina Center
Conference on Shamanism and Alternative Modes of Healing
(photo by Jean Millay)

The Visionary Process

We knowers are unknown to ourselves and for
a very good reason: How can we ever hope
to find what we have never looked for?

Nietzsche (1887/1956:149)

As soon as we become aware of our helplessness, we recognize the need to replenish ourselves and look for the reason of our confusion. Ignorance is, indeed, the cause of all suffering. Sufficiently motivated to remove this ignorance, we begin to look for means to explore our potential.

Our cognition relies on our memory bank. We accumulate memories during our life time, but there are also memories of our ancestors and the knowledge compiled over the centuries by our culture. Imprinted in our DNA, deep inside of us, there are also memories of the Source.

We treat everything that is not scientifically verifiable as if it does not exist. Why do we allow ourselves to be brainwashed into a false complacency? Why don't we look for memories which connect us with the Source?

What has been pushed aside as "non-existing" for so long is now welling up. Just listen!

It should be remembered that we are operating simultaneously on, at least, five levels of experience:

1. the biological-physical,
2. the emotional-psychological,
3. the intellectual-cognitive,
4. the social, and
5. the spiritual.

At times, one level may be more prominent than the others. Each level also stores specific memories, but all levels are intimately connected, all the time. Imbalances may manifest on different levels, so that the ultimate cause of an imbalance may not easily be visible. We have to help each level become aware of the others because the delicate balance between levels of experience is necessary to walk through the "doors of perception" with ease.

It does not matter whether individuals believe in previous lives. It does not matter whether individuals have ever heard of the Akashic Records (by whatever name we want to call them). It does not matter whether individuals uphold certain belief systems which may or may not nourish them. The only thing which matters is that we are sufficiently curious to explore the depth of our own being. It is important that we want to know more about ourselves and "all our relations." What matters is that we accept responsibility for ourselves! What matters is that we are seeking buried treasures — the knowledge which tells us how to lead a meaningful life.

What I am talking about has been expressed before but only a few heard the message. Murphy himself is citing Aurobindo and James who saw "universal evolution arising from a previous involution of Divinity in nature" (1992:190). Philosophers and mystics use parables, aphorisms, or metaphysical statements to express the ineffable.

"Before your parents were," asks a famous Zen koan, "what is your original face?" This celebrated line suggests that we enjoy an essential subjectivity or personhood that precedes our birth and outlasts death itself.

In a famous Hindu parable, a tiger separated since birth from its mother is raised by sheep, believing itself to be one of them until another tiger shows it its own reflection in a river.

We are all tigers, the parable implies, all secretly God (or Brahman) though we think we are something else.

> The Platonic doctrine of anamnesis, or "recollection," which asserts that we can remember the Divine Ideas as underlying sense impressions, is based upon the belief that humans have immortal souls that communed with those Ideas before assuming a mortal body (Murphy, 1992:191-192).

And Huxley reminds us that

> the function of the brain and nervous system and sense organs is in the main eliminative and not productive. Each person is at each moment capable of remembering all that has ever happened to him and of perceiving everything that is happening everywhere in the universe. The function of the brain and nervous system is to protect us from being overwhelmed and confused by this mass of largely useless and irrelevant knowledge, by shutting out most of what we should otherwise perceive or remember at any moment, and leaving only that very small and special selection which is likely to be practically useful....To formulate and express the contents of this reduced awareness, man has invented and endlessly elaborated those symbol-systems and implicit philosophies which we call languages. Every

individual is at once the beneficiary and the victim of the linguistic tradition into which he has been born — the beneficiary inasmuch as language gives access to the accumulated records of other people's experience, the victim in so far as it confirms him in the belief that reduced awareness is the only awareness and as it bedevils his sense of reality, so that he is all too apt to take his concepts for data, his words for actual things (1963:22-23).

We will never forget the moment we caught the first glimpse of the "Light." However, as long as we have a material body, we have to return to the material world where we are tempted into forgetting.

As soon as we have recognized that we have to carry the Light into the darkness, we find also that the shift out of consensus reality into the state where we are "in the flow" is not easy. Breaking through the inertia, we teach ourselves and others the art of awareness. We are the candle which carries the Light.

❦ ❦ ❦

Awareness starts with learning how to "breathe." Using our full capacity for breathing, we release what we have repressed or suppressed, sometimes for a long time. We have to empty and clean the vessel so as not to pour "new wine" into "dirty" receptacles.

While our breath is "sweeping our body" from head to toes, we exhale from the diaphragm. We learn to enjoy the release of used air and, with it, everything which blocks our body, mind, emotion, and soul. This prepares us for drinking the fresh air and feeling our whole body being nourished.

Breathing is rhythmic, whether we breathe fast or slow. Breathing too fast can lead to hyperventilation. For a brief period, it may be very invigorating but, after approximately three minutes of fast breathing, we become "lightheaded." This is not the state in which we work most effectively. Another breathing technique, e.g., in the Yogic tradition, when practiced systematically, "results in prolonged suspensions of breath" which may lead to a high concentration of carbon dioxide in the lungs and blood, and this increase in the concentration of CO_2 lowers the efficiency of the brain as a reducing valve and permits the entry into consciousness of experiences, visionary or mystical, from "out there" (Huxley, 1963:144).

We aim at quieting our mind to increase our awareness; therefore, we breathe slowly but fully and enjoy the ebbing in and out of the breath. Breathing is the first sign of life. When we stop breathing, life stops as well.

❋ ❋ ❋

The next step is to tune ourselves. The method of tuning is taught, for example, by Don Campbell in his Sound School (1991, 1992). To tune yourself is highly effective. But you can also use the purifying sound of a Tibetan bowl which clears and entrains the mind , alleviating mistrust, fostering understanding, and evoking joy. Tuning is the most pleasurable way to interconnect everybody in the range of the sound.

I later added "sonic driving" (Heinze, 1991:157-168; 1988:84-94), because we can use all the help we can get to reconnect to the Source of Information. (The original meaning of religion, religere, is "to tie together again.")

It is essential that you explore different sounds and music (e.g., harpsichord, Zen flute, Gregorian chanting).

You can observe how your body reacts to the different vibrations. To explore this to the fullest, it is recommended to take off your shoes, loosen your belt, and lie quietly on the floor. Uncross your legs and keep your arms relaxed, close to your body.

Being fully tuned, you can then discover your body in dance. Recommended are Indian ragas because they are cyclical and provide at least thirty minutes of rhythmical stimulation. (You need sufficient time for the thorough exploration of your body). In India, ragas are played to express devotion to a deity and, like good medicine, there are specific ragas for each season and each hour of day or night. In a raga, the soul searches for the beloved and the beloved is God. (For those who have problems with the word "God," I suggest you ask yourself what the "beloved" means to you. Be not discouraged, the Divine will appear, disclosing Itself gradually in the process)!

By purifying and reconnecting your body, your mind, emotions, and soul, the conditions for breaking through the layers of misconception are provided (Heinze, 1992:128-136). Expectations arise and "may reduce the number of self-defeating thoughts and images... [and] increase the frequency of coping self-statements and positive images" (Bootzin, 1985). At this point, you begin to discover hidden resources and may find messages waiting for you.

☙ ☙ ☙

For the most important step, I designed a simple structure which borrows some elements from hypnotherapy. However, the session leader should remind all participants to remember each step so that they can later find "their way" on their own, in dreams or other journeys.

After having been led through breathing, relaxation, and tuning exercises, you are invited to mentally go down ten steps, open a door to a room which will serve as a "space station" between the state of consensus reality and other states of consciousness. You are asked to look around in the room and memorize its features so that you can return to it whenever you wish to do so. You can also ask questions at any point of the journey. Then you are invited to go across the room and open a second door which leads to the unknown. You step ou t and close the door behind you. At this point either the sound of a drum or a Tibetan bowl provides the container for the main part of the experience. Sound facilitates the exploration of the unknown. The information, locked in your cells, can be retrieved. The visions you are looking for can be found right inside of you.

※ ※ ※

The exercise has been designed to free the Source from cognitively automatized censorship, i.e., you have to overcome the deficiencies of your cognitive system, to

1. pave a highway into the less conscious regions of your mind which you can improve with each journey and dream, and to
2. access not yet familiar levels of knowing.

In other words, you seek to access information which has been recorded in your body but has not risen to consciousness yet. It may have been

1. held back by the autonomic nervous system to avoid system's overload and/or

2. obscured by grids imposed by family, educational, professional, and societal concerns to filter out so-called "undesirable" information.

Scientists tell us that less than 8% of all incoming information is actually processed. That means that over 92% of all information recorded in your body has not risen to consciousness yet.

What is important for successful reconnection with the Source, when undertaken for the first time, is that this exercise should be facilitated by a professional, experienced not only in information retrieval but prepared also to assist with deep-seated problems which may arise and lead to "spiritual emergencies." "Sonic driving," especially drumming, is bound to trigger the emergence not only of unresolved problems but also of latent trauma and psychoses.

The experience should not be undertaken after a meal. Participants should eat lightly or, even better yet, fast for a few hours and drink only tea or fruit juices. This will help prevent the digestive system from interfering with the flow of information.

Furthermore, in the hours before the experience, participants should refrain from any heavy exercise. They should rest, so that their mind and body are calm when they arrive at the agreed space and time.

1. The facilitator should:
   a. explain the experience to all participants and make sure that all understand the purpose and agree to follow instructions;
   b. give brief and clear instructions, especially about the use of sound (see 7 below);
   c. demonstrate competence and assure all

participants that they are invited into a safe and friendly environment and that they will remember every moment of what transpires (these assurances should be repeated as often as convenient during the event to establish trust and reinforce memory);

d. discourage individuals with a weak ego axis from participation (e.g., warn that suppressed and repressed problems, as well as, latent trauma may come up. The facilitator has to know how to talk such individuals through the "horror," and allow the problem to become the teacher). Participants should also be told that they have the right to withdraw at any time;

e. encourage all to go beyond their consensus reality because the environment of the session is safe and protected and the facilitator will be available at all times.

2. All participants should confirm that:
   a. they have fully understood the nature of the experience,
   b. they are aware of the possibility they may have to deal with unforeseen problems, and
   c. they trust their facilitator.

3. The facilitator has to:
   a. check and prepare the space where the experience will take place. The space should be neutral, non-frightening, non-distracting, soundproof, and purified (e.g., with sage, blessed water, and sound);

    b. tell participants to purify themselves by
        i. washing hands and face with drinking water, and/or
       ii. breathing (progressively, from a sigh of relief to sweeping the body with increased intensity), and/or
     iii. smudging (with sage or incense), or
     iv. all of the above.

4. The facilitator should:
    a. relax everyone, step by step, starting with their toes and ending with the top of their head. Guided relaxation reduces not only physical tensions, it empties the mind and raises expectations. Not only the body but also the mind has to be prepared and alerted so that it can interconnect and become focsed and tuned into the "unknown,"
    b. remind everyone not to use active imagination but suspend judgment, and
    c. invite everybody to visualize an empty movie screen, not knowing what "movie" will be played.

5. During the induction, the facilitator should:
    a. use simple, neutral, words and remind all participants to remember when and how they entered different levels of consciousness so that they can begin to pave a highway into less conscious regions of their mind. They can then access this region on their own, e.g., in their dreams;
    b. suggest not to look for animal or other guardian spirits, which though helpful, may

become crutches, but accept what arises on its own.

6. The experience proper begins with the induction of the facilitator:

    a. you will now go down ten steps of a stairway while I am counting from one to ten. With each step you gradually move away from consensus reality and step into deeper levels of knowing. One — two — three — four — five (you are half way down already) six — seven — eight — nine — ten. You are now standing in front of a door.

    b. observe this door. Have you ever seen this door before? How does it look? What is it made of?

    c. open the door, enter the room and close the door behind you.

    d. observe the room which is now your "space station" between consensus reality and the unknown. You will be able to return to this space station in your dreams. Is there any furniture in the room? What is on the walls? What is on the ceiling? Is there anybody in the room? You can ask questions, such as "Why am I here? Is there any message for me?"

    e. at the other end of the room is a second door. Go to this door and observe how the door looks. What is it made of? Have you ever seen this door before? How is it different from the first door?

    f. open the door, "step out," and close the door behind you.

7. Then the facilitator should sound a Tibetan bowl, a rattle, or a drum for ten minutes. (It is suggested not to use tapes because they don't carry all the vibrations of live sound). The facilitator should also mention that participants can use their breath and the sound of the drum, rattle or Tibetan bowl:

   a. as a weapon to ward off negativity. If something frightening appears, go toward it. It might change; if not, go past it;

   b. to overcome obstacles (going through walls, etc.);

   c. to ride the sound, and when nothing seems to be happening, to be patient, to trust, and simply allow yourself to be carried by the sound;

   d. to stay in the moment and observe, but not change (produce) anything mentally;

   e. to ask questions when something becomes unclear. Some answers may be clear, some may emerge in symbolic form and have to be interpreted, and sometimes you may have to say, "come again";

   f. not to enter the journey with a previously fixed question because it will block out any new information.

8. After ten minutes of sound, the facilitator should talk the participants through their return journey, using the same words with which s/he had led them into the experience:

   a. remember what you have experienced and feel good about it. Then go back to the second door.

b. open the second door, step across the threshold, and close the door behind you. You are now back in the room (space station). Have a last look at the room. Is it still the same room? Or has it changed? Remember the experience and feel good about it.

c. go back to the first door, open it, step across the threshold, and close the door behind you. You see now the ten steps in front of you.

d. climb up the ten steps, one by one, while I am counting back from ten to one: Ten— nine — eight — seven — six. You are half up already; remember everything and feel good about it. Five — four — three — two — one.

e. you are now back in the room from where we started.

9. Participants should be encouraged to write down the experience immediately after the session, because our "conscious" mind tends to change content over time. The many grids imposed on us by culture, family, professional and peer groups will try to "desensitize" and corrupt the content.

10. The experience should also be processed with all participants before they leave. Though sharing is voluntary, participants should be encouraged to talk about their experience, because the recollection reinforces memory.

❧ ❧ ❧

At the time of recollecting the experience, it is useful to resort to active imagination, amplification, etc., to facilitate the search for meaning. The message has to "feel right." Participants may have to seek clarification in asking questions in their dreams and/or they may have to go onto another journey.

The facilitator has to take care of any problems arising and offer assistance, so that whatever transpired can be brought to full consciousness and resolved. The facilitator should, under no circumstances, suggest solutions but should encourage exploring possible alternatives. This part requires training and experience, especially with "spiritual emergencies."

Important messages and visions will come with such clarity that they leave no doubt. When there are doubts, participants should go with the doubt and check whether expectations or wishful thinking may have clouded the experience. The mind may have been unwilling to stay in the observer position or it may have refused to accept the information.

Some of us need more preparations to understand the exercise and need more assistance in shifting attention. Facilitator and participants should also look together at interferences which may have sidetracked the traveler. If blocks that prevent the flow of information can be discovered and removed, comprehension of the experience can be greatly enhanced.

Participants may have to try again, until the mirror of the Inner Source becomes clear and radiant and they enter the subtle but pervading state of Creative Joy. The information is inside of you. Be patient! In your search for knowledge, patience is the main ingredient.

❀ ❀ ❀

The above exercise can be modified to serve more specific goals:

HEALING

The facilitator uses the same induction up to point 6c, and then describes the room as an

1. open hall, surrounded by mountains which can be seen in the distance. Water is springing out of the mountains. Jugs with fresh mountain water have been put next to the place whe re you decide to lie down — on the soft grass or the simple beds which have been provided for this purpose. You are invited to rest wherever you feel comfortable.
2. lean back, once in a while pour yourself some water from the jugs. While you are drinking the water, you feel the freshness of the mountain water pervading your body.
3. while you are lying in the open, basking in the invigorating sun, relaxing and contemplating the landscape, take another sip from the nourishing water, whenever you feel like it..
4. soft winds arise and, with each breeze, you feel its energy flowing into your body. Each breeze also carries away some blockages and pain you may have. It feels as if the pain, slowly but surely, is dusted away with a silken handkerchief.

After having set the scene, the facilitator uses the sound of a Tibetan bowl. Each ring of the bowl reinforces the imagery and the healing.

After ten minutes of healing sound, participants are told to remember everything and to feel good about it. They are then led back through the first door (note, that a second door is never mentioned). They are asked to consciously close the door behind them and climb up the ten stairs, while the facilitator counts back from ten to one.

The experience should be written down immediately. Though sharing is always optional, recollection should be encouraged because it reinforces memory.

Participants should be told that they can return to this open hall in their dreams so that they may drink more of the healing water and feel the breeze carrying away their pain.

RETRIEVAL OF SPECIFIC INFORMATION

The facilitator uses the same induction technique to point 6c and describes the room as a

1. library where all knowledge is stored. There is a book on the table and you are invited to go and read the page to which the book has been opened, and
2. if you are not satisfied with what you have read, you may want to turn the pages to other parts of the book or get up and select another book, until you feel you have received a satisfactory message.

The facilitator then uses the sound of a drum, rattle or a Tibetan bowl for ten minutes. After ten minutes, participants are told to remember everything and feel good about it.

They are asked to go back to the door and consciously close the door behind them. They are the

n invited to climb up the ten stairs, while the facilitator is counting back from ten to one.

The experience should be written down and shared
with all present after the event. Though sharing is
optional, recollection reinforces memory.

❦ ❦ ❦

A satisfactory message may not be found easily.
Sometimes your conscious mind blocks the entrance
to the Source for a long time. The facilitator should
then invite you to relax, lie down again and wait until
the information rises on its own. It is quite possible that messages may emerge sometime after the
session, when you are in a more relaxed mood.

You can also recall the experience before you go to
sleep and invite your dreams to clarify the issue.

The question may have to be reformulated or your
concern more clearly expressed, so that a new journey can be undertaken on another day when you are
better prepared.

Between journeys, contemplation and meditation,
music, as well as, dancing will soften conscious barriers and increase awareness.

Quieting your mind to reach the state of "deep
reflection" and being patient, will become easier, after
the first satisfactory results have been obtained.

❦ ❦ ❦

You will feel it immediately when the information fits.
"Realness" is not doubted though the "feeling of realness"
may not be "correlated with corresponding variability in
the [consensus] reality" (Deikman, 1969:35).

When messages arise in unknown form, you have to
be reminded that it takes time until meaning emerges
from under the heaps of dust you have piled up on

your best qualities. You may have to look for symbols and metaphors suitable to carry ineffable information. It requires patience to become "clear as glass." You will decipher the message as soon as you are ready for it.

Once again I strongly suggest that when you want to explore less conscious levels of knowing and decide to use "sonic driving," you should ask somebody to be present during the experience:

1. until you have become familiar
   a. with your problems (suppressed and repressed emotional trauma), and
   b. with the nature and sequence of steps toward connecting, and
2. until you have paved highways into the less conscious regions of your mind,

it is prudent to ask a professional facilitator for assistance. Even the most experienced shamans and mediums I worked with during the last thirty-five years in Asia had family or community members present, ready to assist during trance. It was the task of the helpers to facilitate the entrance into the trance state and to assist with the exit, back to ordinary reality. A wide range of unforeseeable factors can influence the nature of the experience. The above exercise is bound to touch suppressed and repressed material which will not only cause discomfort but can activate latent psychoses requiring lifelong care.

As an example, I want to share the story of a woman who got "stuck in the mouth of a snake." During her journey, she had entered the snake by its tail. Traveling through the snake's body, she discovered that the snake would not open its mouth. Stuck behind the snake's teeth, she had not enough strength to move further. I had to relax the "snake" which then willingly opened its mouth and the woman emerged relieved but shaken. Her anxiety needed to be taken care of, i.e., she needed the presence of an assistant, before she could move out of the experience.

At another time, a participant fell into a deep, so-called "possession," trance. I gently called his name until I got a faint muscular response. Working with this response, I talked the young man through the trance, asking him to follow my voice. I also gently tapped the so-called third eye (the spot between the eye brows) and massaged the diaphragm. Dissociations may happen deeper than expected; therefore, the process I described should not be used without preparation and without a professional assistant standing by.

It is vital to have a

1. supportive environment (free of interferences and purified in the ways described above),
2. supportive and experienced person nearby,
3. pure and open mind, and a
4. deep desire to explore and be nourished by the Source.

Any anxiety will disturb the experience. If there is any indication that serious problems or unconscious trauma may arise, I strongly suggest that a professional should be consulted first whether it is advisable to go on a "journey." Before journeys can be experienced safely, a professional can, for example, suggest breathing exercises and give Reiki treatments which proved to be very successful in the case on which I reported at the end of "My Story."

❀ ❀ ❀

The above technique offers a safe structure for all who want to explore their state of being. But, most of all, the technique leads to finding the information you need to lead a satisfactory life.

❀ ❀ ❀

In the next part I will present twenty cases, selected from a sample of over a thousand. The stories show what can be reclaimed when we open the "doors of perception."

There are, however, many other "doors" and in Part III, I will describe seven of them.

I intentionally did not talk about psychoactive drugs. They certainly offer glimpses into new dimensions but also carry the risk of creating dependencies.

I did not talk about vision quests. For vision quests, you need proper preparations (which take more than one day) and you also have to find good teachers to protect the process.

Join in the Dance!

Ruth's Favorite Image: Dancing Shiva

Visionary Experiences

The spiritual does not vary from time to time
because it is not within time.
Spirit is unchanging.
A deep sense of the spiritual leads one
not to trust one's own lonely power
but the great flow or pattern manifested
in all life, including our own.
We become not manipulator but witness.

Rachel Naomi Remen (1993:41)

The "process" is universal. I will now introduce you to excerpts from the over thousand stories I collected at my workshops during the last seven years in the United States, Russia, Lithuania, and Estonia.

When you learn to shift your attention from the ordinary world to other levels of consciousness, you can, like Alice in Wonderland, go through the Looking Glass and find yourself in the reflection. William James suggested that we

> plunge...into an altogether other dimension of existence from the sensible and merely "understandable" world. Name it the mystical region, or the supernatural region....So far as our ideal impulses originate in this region... we belong to it in a more intimate sense than that in which we belong to the visible world.... Yet the unseen region...is not merely ideal, for it produces effects in this world. When we commune with it, work is actually done upon our finite personality.... But that which produces effects within another reality must be termed a reality itself so I feel as if we had no philosophic excuse for calling the unseen or mystical world unreal (1961:388-389).

Contemplation and meditation increase your awareness and refine the mechanism of your consciousness. Music and dance express your inner feelings. When you open up and become whole and light, you can breathe with the universe.

The process changed my life because I could access deeper levels of knowing. We all can become "little hollow bones" (Fools Crow/Mails, 1991) who want to share the joy of "dancing in the middle of the stream."

As an actress I manifested a wide range of conflicts and emotions and led the audience into cathartic resolutions, be it through tears or, even better, through laughter. Actors learn how to "project," how to tune their audience not only with their voice, but also with their emotions, their mind, their soul and, don't forget, their body. On stage, meaning is conveyed not only with words. Meaning is manifested "in the flesh." Being is more convincing than words. Devoted teachers have known this since time immemorial.

I did not mention any specific religion to avoid dogmatic controversy. The simple exercise I suggest works in any religious framework, whether it is a world religion or a local belief system. I speak for all who want to explore the different levels of their consciousness. I speak for those who want to connect with the Source, by whatever name they call It—God, Allah, Brahma, Wakan Tanka, the Akashic Records, the Divine.

I did not mention praying. In prayer we are asking for the fulfillment of wishes, for blessing, protection, and grace. We all need grace, but grace is only granted when the time is right. Some of us think they can buy grace with "good" deeds. They expect to be rewarded for exemplary behavior. Grace, however, cannot be coerced in any way.

You cannot expect Divine intervention whenever you need it. You have to put your feet firmly on this earth and focus on techniques which increase awareness of yourself and of "all your relations." Such awareness changes your life completely and keeps you moving toward a goal beyond your highest expectations.

Before I report how these "journeys" affected those looking for knowledge and information, I want to discuss briefly dependency needs. If we observe ourselves closely, we recognize that we all have certain dependencies, far beyond childhood. We continue to feel entitled to protection and nourishment. Those who want security and to be taken care of all their lives, are never satisfied, and attach themselves to and expect to live through others. They do not want to move themselves. Good teachers foster independence, even though independence is not what most people want.

When you are looking for advice and encouragement, for love and protection, teachers will not always be available in critical moments. You may also question whether a certain teacher is right for you. In this case, reliance on yourself is undoubtedly better than being drawn into a direction which is wrong for you. You can, however, prepare yourself for moments of uncertainty and darkness. The process I suggest works well at any time.

The problem starts with the fact that a surprisingly large number of people do not trust themselves. If they do not trust themselves, then how can they trust others or be trusted by others? Clearing their mind, their intentions, and their emotions, they have to find themselves first.

It is important to start the search with a pure mind and pure intentions. It is also important not to expect anything specific. During the whole process, you have to tell your mind to remain in the observer position. You have to tell your discursive thoughts not to interfere. I am definitely not denigrating thinking. You have to remember what has transpired and have to think about how you want to process the experience. However, discursive thinking during a transcendent experience blocks the flow necessary for creative and unusual feats. I am reinforced here, for example, by Murphy who, when discussing extraordinary physical feats, quotes Shainberg as saying: "that sensorimotor commands operate more efficiently" when "unimpeded by unnecessary mental activity"(1992:119).

Yes, we need our mind as an observer in the process of learning but what needs to be learned, in the first place, is to trust the "substance."

The following twenty cases from past workshops will now illustrate the process.

❦ ❦ ❦

CASE ONE

After a drumming journey in Berkeley, California, 1987, a woman in her sixties reported:

> I entered a tunnel. Far ahead, I saw the light at the end of the tunnel which naturally (not man-made) wound through the mountain. I kept moving fast but the tunnel turned out to be longer than expected. I could not see day light anymore. There was darkness all around me. I kept moving faster and faster and realized that I was traveling to the womb of the earth.
>
> Finally, a reddish glow appeared in the distance. The glow increased and turned out to be

magma — molten rock, the fiery womb of the earth. The rock I had traveled through began to melt and I decided to enter the magma. The fiery heat strengthened my bones. I felt the lava flowing through my veins and rose with it to the surface. In a cloud of steam, the lava flowed into the sea while I stepped onto the beach.

There was a cave on the beach. I realized that a dragon lived in the cave. I challenged the dragon to come out, but he did not stir. I repeated my challenge and he teased me by first showing part of his right paw, then a pointed ear, and then part of his back. I told him to stop the nonsense and the dragon finally came out. He still clowned around, rolling his eyes and looking cross-eyed at me. He began to dance and spat neat little lightning bolts into every direction. I told him again to stop the foolishness and the dragon rolled in laughter. He said, "Don't you know I am you and you are me? Don't you spit fire like me? You even have a big belly like me." I found his remark rather impolite and reminded him that he was supposed to tell me something, but the dragon kept laughing and changing his shape. He changed into a turtle, a phoenix, and an elephant, saying, "Remember, I was also the elephant you rode in Nepal."

Finally, I could persuade the dragon to engage in some useful activities and we decided to clean up the environment. We flew over the land and spat fire. Everything which had fulfilled its purpose and had become useless was consumed

by the fire. The clean ashes made the land
fertile again.

After a while, we called it a day and the dragon
showed me how to get out of deep tunnels
so I would not get stuck in them anymore.
We returned to the womb of the earth and he
pointed to the windows on the cave roof. Each
window led into a different reality.

Looking at the contents of this vision, it seems that
when we decide to enter the path toward self-cultivation,
we first have to deal with basic fears. They prevent us
from exploring the unknown. We hardly know ourselves, so we continue to search for natural tunnels
which lead to the deeper layers of our mind. We cultivate our faculty to reach the core in which every form
is molten down and dissolved in the "Cosmic Fire."

Metzner (1986:59-74) talks about the purification by
inner fire. Fire and light are surrounding us and are also
deep inside of us. This fiery center of all things then has
the power to propel us back to the surface. In fact, it
sends us, over and over again, back to everyday reality.
Only after we have fulfilled our task, is our ego allowed
to be molten down to "no-thing-ness" where there is
nothing but the brilliant light of formlessness.

Arthur Young reminds us that,

Light, because it is primary, must be *unqual-
ified*—*impossible to describe*—because it is anteced-
ent to the contrast necessary to description.

...it has *no mass*...no charge and, as evidenced by
the finding of relativity that clocks stop at the

speed of light, it has *no time*...and *cannot be at rest*. Even *space* is a *meaningless* concept for light, since the passage of light through space is accomplished without any loss of energy whatsoever.

Light involves us in a special kind of difficulty, the difficulty about that which provides our knowledge of other things...light by which we see, cannot be seen...Light is not seen, *it is seeing* (1976:10-11).

Like students, told to do their "home work," we are told to carry the message, the "inner knowledge" (which is pure light), into our "surface consciousness" over and over again.

In the vision, the fiery lava did not immediately take the woman back to everyday reality. She was spilled on a beach where a mythical dragon lived. Dragons are transformational animals in many cultures. Rain-bearing clouds, for example, are considered to be such dragons. Look how the dragon spits lightning before the rain! Dragons appear where fire and water meet. This dragon taught the woman how to recognize some of some of her shapes and how to discover, "hidden ones." He reminded her that our "being" is more than what conforms to the name given us by society. He also taught her how to utilize this fire to clear the ground for new growth; he showed new tunnels and windows to different realities.

✾ ✾ ✾

Case Two

A physicist at a retreat house on a hill near Pescadero, California, reported in September 1989:

Ruth's drumming was soft and lulling and rhythmic.... I was already off on other paths....I suddenly received the image of a white bird....I got on the bird and was taken high in the sky over the vast distance — to my father's grave site on Cape Cod. I saw the gray granite plaque with a Star of David made out of twigs.

I then saw my father rise up from the grave, ghostlike, and the message was: he had accepted his death and my mother has freed him, allowing him to rise. He, too, has freed himself from his ties to her, which had been keeping him from claiming his spirit-hood.

I felt, too, that...he wasn't physical anymore, he would be freed from the illness and suffering that had overtaken him in his later years. I hoped that my dreams of him would now change to ones where he is healthy again.

This was a "tearful experience" for her. She continued crying when she shared the journey with the group. The next day, she found six twigs on the path to the hill next to the retreat center. These twigs looked exactly like the ones in her vision. She put them into her father's goblet and later arranged them in the form of the Star of David.

There had not been any stimulus other than the ten minutes of rhythmic drumming. The tiredness of the physicist after a long day of professional discussions made it possible for her to follow the drum beat without any interference by discursive thoughts. The message from beyond the grave was finally heard. The "right" circumstances (the "opening") had occurred naturally.

The image arose spontaneously as if it had waited for this moment of relaxed attention. It had been her first journey.

⁕ ⁕ ⁕

Case Three

After a drumming session in Salt Lake City in August 1991, a middle-aged woman reported:

> Everything happened with a great deal of urgency. I was just caught up by the drum. I started down by the edge of the water and ran up to where I could see the opening of the cave....

> I became a green and gold snake that began to spiral around and around. I spiraled down into the earth. I was very long with no arms but filled with enormous energy: spiraling, spiraling, spiraling down.

> When I got down, I started doubling back and curled up, almost like a Gordian's knot. Then I backed out, through myself, like shedding my skin, and was myself again.

> I was on a beach and saw this small vortex. I was swirling, thinking that the hole might go away before I got to it. So I jumped in.

> I came out in water. I was under water. I was a fish for a time and then I became myself again, swimming along with the fish. I was perfectly comfortable in the water. Then I came shooting out like I was a tidal wave—just enormous energy!

After I had shot out, I found that I was turning into a large cat, like a leopard. I was racing
across this big plain, racing and racing.

Then I came to this huge tree where the branches
seemed to have been knocked off. I ran straight up
the tree—higher and higher and higher—until
I was so high it was unbelievable.

I looked down and it was far too high to come
back down again. So, I thought that what I had
better do is snap this tree off at the base. I started
to sway back and forth, again and again, to snap
the tree but it was far too resilient. Then I just
pulled back and flipped myself off.

I turned into a bird! I was a seagull and I could fly.

She commented later: "So this is the message: I
thought that I was aiming too high, that I was trying
to get too high, that my aspirations were too great. I
thought I was going to have to snap off and go back to
the base, but once I got to the top of the tree, I knew
I could fly. I can fly!"

Earlier in the workshop, some physical problems
seemed to restrict her movements. She also had voiced
severe doubts about her energy level. Her liberating
report speaks for itself. It was the strongest reaction
I witnessed so far during many years of facilitating
drumming journeys. She swam, she raced across the
plain, and she could fly. Yes, she could fly!

The experience surprised her, as well as, everybody
present. Her exuberance was physically visible. She had
shifted into a new mode of action, so much so that,

immediately after, she embarked on a series of new activities. Her energy had, indeed, "unexpectedly" risen from the depth!

✦ ✦ ✦

Case Four

In September 1992, a middle-aged woman at an international conference held in San Raphael, California, wrote after a drumming journey,

> I couldn't get into the room at the bottom of the basement stairs. It was very dark and I searched through caverns for a door, but everything was purple and misty. Finally I turned my head toward the light, and beams of sunlight spread all around me. There were garlands, wreaths, flowers, especially a camellia and hollyhocks. It seemed that I was lying outside in the garden.

> Images came to me in triangles with small pictures of abstract art inside, mostly Modigliani, cubist paintings, several in Picasso style, but also one of Whistler's mother. The scenes moved very fast.

> I saw a huge sun-like phenomenon coming toward me and hovering over me. I even saw writing on it in small letters. It seemed that some mystical truth was being imparted, and I tried to get closer to read it. I opened my eyes just slightly and saw that the brilliant sun above me was really the bottom side of the chair I was lying under.

> I turned my head away, and it grew darker. I was stumbling through curtains into a huge

opera house which was only partially revealed to me. Chandeliers and velvet curtains were all around me. I was searching for a place to sit, but nothing was available.

Then we were told to go into the next room and observe. I still couldn't see the door, but was somehow transported into a room filled with arches, ancient ruins, all the colors of desert sand. There were Phoenician-like figures and designs. I began examining one very profound-looking, dignified statue of a humanized bird, but then we were told to leave.

I searched frantically for a way out, then turned my head back to the light and suddenly was back in the room. I checked under the chair to see if there really was writing. It was the manufacturer's name.

The woman could not quiet her intellect. Her discursive thinking prevented a clearer view of deep-seated images. The statue of a "humanized bird" did not come alive. She needed more journeys to trust herself until she could explore her "Inner Source" without intellectual interference. We have to cultivate our curiosity to become a discoverer and tell the researcher inside of us not to pre-judge the images which have messages for us.

It is interesting that, despite the distractions, she saw a triangle, and other loaded symbols, with which she can work on later.

? ? ?

Case Five
In 1993, at a Rainbow Horse Dance in Cazadero, a

mother who had lost her 19-year-old son, one year ago in a motorcycle accident, wanted to "check her mailbox." He had been her only child and she was still grieving about the loss but had managed to keep herself together until Mother's Day (which would have been his 20th birthday).

She began her journey by going down

> the roots of a huge bay tree on my beach [her special place for visualization]. Down gray marble circular stairs. Down, down, down. I was looking at them from far away. Randy [her son] appeared as a guide. We went down, down, down, far away. I was there, instead of observing from afar.

> We went into a dark room. A medicine man appeared, dressed in orange colors. He danced around me while Randy watched. The shaman manifested a red-hot poker and stuck it through my heart.

> I writhed with agony. "Love it—embrace it. You will learn from it," I was directed. I did so and it melted away....

> The poker reappeared as a sword. I was also given a crystal ball. Then, I was given a task: I had to fight/slay a white monster dragon. I did so easily. I was scared first but it was only fear; it wasn't hard to do at all.

> Then I had to fight/slay Nazis. Here they came. I sent out protection and love. They melted

away....All that was left were gold nuggets on the floor.

I was instructed to ritually bathe for healing. I went to another area where there was a pool filled with sparkling, celestial water. I immersed myself with the sword in my right hand and the crystal ball in my left.

As we went beneath the water, the sword and the crystal ball were absorbed into my arms. My hands got very hot at this point.

Then we went home.

Going through the pain of losing her son, she found a way to heal herself and felt reconnected.

✿ ✿ ✿

CASE SIX

At the Rainbow Horse Dance at Cazadero, California, September 1993, a young woman reported,

it was a little hard at the beginning with all the distractions [we were lying under the trees behind the retreat center and people would ride by and talk]. After going down the ten steps (of which I have no real recollection), I came to an old wooden door (it was a strong door).

When I opened the door, there was no other room. I was in space. It was like a dark void. Not totally black—lots of twinkling stars—like the universe. It reminded me of all the energy I see in the darkness when I concentrate on it. It felt good. I felt at home in this place and I really did not wish to materialize another door.

As I tried to visualize the second door, I barely saw a glass door, only the top half.

After I went through this door, I had a hard time seeing anything. I liked the first room better. All the images reminded me of a snowy image you get on a TV screen at times. I tried to relax and let the images flow, remembering what you had told me.

I felt I was sitting on a grassy hill, overlooking many other grassy hills below. The grass seemed to be semi-dry but still with a hint of green left. There was a breeze.

I felt as though there were prayer items around me which reminded me of South Dakota, the Pine Ridge Reservation. There seemed to be poles with feathers and tobacco ties. Not right in my vision, but next to me; I could not see, but felt them. It was like a vision quest. Perhaps only the images of an inner dream and goal of mine.

I felt the drums were coming from my village below. I became very sad because I missed these times and their memories. I began to fill up with tears. I would have cried like a baby. The sadness was very deep inside my heart. I pulled away from it and tried to relax again.

There were still no vivid images. At one time, I barely saw the image of an old white-haired Indian. His hair was blown by the wind and he seemed suspended in the air. (He looked like one of Frank Howell's paintings). I only saw his face from the nose up.

He brought both of his hands to his mouth and blew something to me.

I remember recalling my life as it is today. How involved I have become with native ways: the path to knowledge, ritual, friends and politics. I felt good, everything was natural for me. And here I was lying on the forest floor, listening to the drums. Also, how I felt haunted with some memory of another life time, trying to understand my connection to native ways and this path I have been traveling for so long.

Then I knew that I was doing all that I could, right at this time in my life. That everything is

in place, kept in balance, one moment at a time.
After this the drumming stopped.

She was not sufficiently relaxed to go to deeper levels,
so she went with the sound of the drum. It brought up
Native American memories and, in the middle of the
imagery, the message arose that "everything is in place,"
and all she had to do was keep the balance and take "one
moment at a time."

❦ ❦ ❦

Case Seven

A woman, in her thirties, at a retreat in Oakville,
California, 1994, reported:

I went down the wide, shallow stone stairs
in a park near my mother's house in Ohio. I
hiked many times in this park and had many
significant dreams about it. They are some of
the most mysterious, symbolic, and real stairs I
know. They go down to a real river and through
a real glacial gorge where I have climbed since
my adolescence. They are "my" stairs.

When I got to the bottom, I was no longer in the park, but at the entrance to Carlsbad Caverns. The first room was the first large room of Carlsbad. There was no one there. I was alone. It was mostly dark, but I could still see. It was cool, but comfortable. I began to feel fear at being alone, so far below ground, but your talking reminded me this was the beginning, not the end of the journey.

The next door was also into a different room of the cave. The stalactites on the ceiling were dripping water. The walls were rich sandstone and water was running down in places. There were rock curtains where minerals had calcified, and there were stalagmites around the perimeter, like huge candlesticks. I was still alone. There was no one. I was becoming afraid again. The door behind me was closed; the door in front of me was closed.

When I had to open the second door, it was a long time before I could step out into the complete darkness. I did not know if the next step was level ground, up a hill, or a drop of a few inches, or a foot, or into an abyss. I hesitated. I looked out into the darkness. I lifted my right foot many times, but I could not step forward. I felt stuck. There was no going forward, but there was no going back either.

I thought, at that moment, about my house with its three steps down to the bedroom, which I have tripped on in the darkness, trying not to disturb my husband or daughter who were sleeping. I thought of my fear that, carrying my daughter to her bed, I might fall and hurt her. I thought of the labyrinth of stairs between my house and the guest house and the number of times I have stumbled in the dark before I knew just how many steps there were at each level and turn. And even so, I am always hesitant in the dark—I always test with my foot to see if there might be one more step I have neglected to remember. It makes for maddeningly slow progress, but a mistake, is even worse.

Finally, I stepped out. It was dark and down, and I was still very alone. I was in the dark. Then there was a cold, bright room and I was lying on an operating table, scared and alone. The drumming was strong and steady. It was all I could hear. It was my heart pounding in my ears. I was on the operating table with toxemia. My blood pressure was in the stroke range. I knew that I might die at any moment and my baby was far too young to be born, let alone survive. I feared for the torture which I knew awaited her if there was to be a chance. I prayed it would be a girl, because I knew girl babies did better in these circumstances than boys. I was so relieved finally to be on my back after ten days on my left side. The lights were too bright and the people there were maintaining that awful silence that medical people keep when the shit is really about to hit the fan, but they don't want to alarm the patient. I knew that if I did not control my emotions, the fear would raise the blood pressure and I might die or become severely disabled from a stroke or kidney or liver failure. I was lying there in the sorrowful company of women who died in childbirth.

At this point, the drumming was becoming more and more intense. I was crying; streams of tears were falling from both eyes down my temples into my ears. The real fears were back, in my mind, my soul, my body. I came back from the vision, and considered whether I could get up and leave the room without disrupting the others. I decided I couldn't.

I went back to the operating room in my mind. I was still there, I was being cut on. I could feel the pain through the light anesthetic. It hurt. I hurt. I was as afraid as I have ever been. I was as afraid in the vision as I was at the real operation. No, I was more afraid. More afraid because I knew it was the drum and not my heart. It was not the disease. It was Ruth-Inge drumming. The pain was real, the fear was real. What happened to me three years ago was real. I had forgotten even less than I had hoped I would have by now. Would I ever be free of this? Would I ever stop crying?

The drum was most intense now. Why doesn't she just stop or at least back off? Why can't I forget? I want to get out of here. I want a different vision to happen. I want the nightmares of the last three years never to have happened. I didn't need this kind of self-knowledge. I certainly didn't need it intruding now. I became more and more angry. And the drum still beat.

I couldn't separate from the memories, from the fear. It happened to me. It happened to me. It happened to me. There were four other people in the room that day, but the nightmare happened to me. No matter how much good will and hope was being sent my way, I was doing the suffering. No one else could do this for me. And now again on this mat, in this living room. Would I ever be free of this? Probably not. So I'd best start coping. Damn. I really don't want to.

Hear the drum. It's a drum. A drum. A drum. Try to ride it. Drum surfing. Go with the sound. See where else it can take you. You've been to the worst you have to offer yourself. Any place else has to be better. Ride it. Ride it. Ride it. Go. Go. Go....Sound surfing. Be the drum. Become the beat. You are no longer the drum, you are the sound. Pulsing. Tensing, relaxing. Tensing, relaxing. Breathing, flowing, moving.

On top of the sound. It is beneath me. I can ride it like a wave. I float on it, feel it rocking, beneath me. It's farther away now. I am above it. It is below, but there to support me if I should sink. I don't think. I don't think so. I begin to laugh. A full belly laugh. I smile. I giggle quietly. I don't care who sees me or what they think.

It is green. The grass is green. The trees have leaves. It is spring, May. Life has burst forth. I am dancing to the beat of life. It is individual. It is harmony. It is one. I begin to dance, I am turning clockwise. There are pastel colored streamers emanating from my white Greek dress. I am twirling clockwise. My feet touch the ground lightly and firmly at the same time. The dance is strong. I am the beat. I am the May pole. The streamers dance around me. The other dancers are the Life in the meadow. It has no body; it is there, permeating everything. I begin to laugh again. I am having a great time. Life is good. Life is joy. It feels good to smile and laugh from the soul.

I begin to dance more forcefully. I am Shiva, with many arms, dancing, stamping the creation into being. I am stamping on the earth: Wake up! Be solid! Be real! I am dancing a few feet above the ground. Step lightly, keep the beat, do no harm. I continue to twirl clockwise; the streamers are deep lavender, pastel orange, blue, pink, I am spinning into myself. I expand beyond my own body, and for a time become one with the Life that is here.

For some unknown time, I simply am, I am whole. I am active and still. I am. There is no here or there. The drum has disappeared. There is no sound or silence. All is full.

Ruth-Inge is calling us. It is time to begin to come back. I touch lightly on the ground. I am myself, but changed. I walk back to the door. I go into the dark cave. It is the same as before. I am still alone, but I am no longer afraid of either the dark, or the aloneness, or myself. I am empowered to be me in the fullest sense. And I have no care or concern about what that might mean. For now it is simply enough to know.

I walk back into the first room. It seems lighter, more friendly. I am still alone, but stronger. I walk back up the stairs, into the forest. When it is time to open our eyes, I am happy to be in Mary Ann's living room with my friends, I have no sorrow at leaving the vision because, like my private journey to the door of death, I now have a new journey-vision to balance it. I have been through the Door of Life. It has come through me. I have danced it. I have been it. And now I have this knowledge that will no more leave me than the other.

The message I received was that I did not have to be so afraid any more, neither did the women who were gathered for this day.

This journey shows a wide range of emotional development. She started with familiar scenes which led to facing past traumas she had to deal with. She remembered, however, that she could use the drum. She overcame her aversion to its driving force and rode the sound until she was able to dance freely and joyfully the "Dance of Creation."

CASE EIGHT

A young woman at a focus group during a residential retreat reports:

I descend the ten steps and arrive at the door at the bottom. It is mahogany and has six beveled, square panels cut into the wood: two panels, each in three rows. The door is similar to my front door at home, but has fewer panels. The door knob is modern but made out of gold.

I enter a round room. On all sides are windows, starting half way up the wall to the top. Through the windows I see darkness and stars. Under the windows are couches or lounge chairs — very plush, like velvet, soft looking, a deep magenta color. The floor is carpeted in a gray color. In the middle of the room, arranged in two semi-circles, are two curved couches, facing each other with walking space between them. The couches are equidistant, so are the windows. The room appears to be divided into thirds. The ceiling is arched over the tops of the walls, in a blue color.

Across from the door by which I entered is another door. It is arched and made of white marble. I do not see a door knob or any latch. I cross the room, between the couches, push the marble door open, and go through it.

I am on a covered porch with columns. I go down the steps from the porch into a garden. Looking back, I see a Greek Temple, white (an almost blinding white) with columns across the porch. The garden is very beautiful. While there is a lot of sunlight and it is very bright, there is no sense of too much heat. It feels just right.

The garden is full of many flowers, trees and birds. However, it does not appear as though it has been planted with any structure in mind, more like it was allowed to grow wild, but structured itself so that not one thing was predominant or out of hand. The colors seem exceptionally bright and the songs of the birds very vivid. It is very peaceful here.

I see a path that is overgrown by the trees on either side. The path itself does not have any growth, only from the sides. I start pushing through the trees to go down the path but suddenly realize that this is not the way I should be doing things in this place. I bow and politely ask that the path be cleared. The trees pull back their limbs and the path becomes clear.

I walk down the path and come to a round clearing with a small, round pool in the middle of it. The clearing has very green and lush grass growing down to the pool. The pool is edged with stone. I reach down and take some water in my right hand, raise it to my mouth, and drink. It is very cold, so cold that I cannot taste it. I only experience the coldness.

I look into the water and see steps leading down within the water, i.e., there are no steps above the water, only under the water. Somehow, it really amazes me to see those steps, as if they are out of character to be there. I step into the water and go down.

It is very dark and I am surprised that I seem to have no trouble breathing. I get to the bottom of the steps and find myself in a tunnel with stone walls. It is cool in the tunnel, but the air is fresh. I get the feeling that it is a maze of some sort, with all the tunnels curving this way and that, but I have no difficulty finding my way.

At the end of the tunnel I come out into a round room made of stone. There is a fireplace on one side with a fire burning in it. In front of the fireplace is an old woman dressed in a soft long dark dress. She has white hair and is very old, I ask her who she is, but she does not answer me. She only looks at me with a direct gaze. She walks out a door onto a balcony surrounded by a stone wall that is about waist high. The balcony is high up and overlooks the Greek temple and the pool. I recognize that the room and the balcony are part of a turret in an English-style castle.

I attempt to talk to the old woman again, but she jumps on the balcony and motions me to follow. She turns into a crow and flies off. I fly off with her, but as myself. We fly into space. It is very black, but shimmering somehow. The blackness is also dense. She turns back into an old woman and shows me how to do something. It has to do with turning sideways around what seems to be a curved surface, and then turning into other odd directions, sideways around other curved surfaces; somehow going from one place to another. I hear the word "dimensionality" in my mind. She motions me to do it. I cannot. So she does it again. This time I can follow her. I almost grasp what she is doing, but I'm not sure if I could do it on my own.

We turn to go back to the castle and I find that I have turned into a crow. When we get back inside the room (in the castle with the fireplace), I am not a crow any longer and neither is the old woman. I again ask the old woman who she is. She says that she is part of me. I ask her if there is any particular knowledge I should be using. She says that there is something for me to do, but then I can't understand what she is saying. I can hear the words, but cannot understand the meaning. Finally, she shows me an image of the place out in space, overlaid, transparent with the maze-like tunnels under the castle. I still do not understand what she is trying to tell me.

I hear the call to return to my waking self. I would have liked to have remained, but I go back into the tunnels. I notice that I do not seem to go down out of the castle, to get to the tunnels; nor do I remember going up into the castle from the tunnels. I just step out of the door of the castle directly into a tunnel. I go through the tunnel, back up the steps, and through the pool of water. I want to take another drink of the water, but hear a voice that says "not now." I go down the path onto the porch of the Greek temple and pass through the door.

The temple door leads into the round room as before. Nothing has changed, except the arched ceiling which, I notice, has become exceptionally brilliant blue turquoise, almost neon in brightness. As I come to the door leading to the steps up, it is not solid. It is like mist. I pass through and turn to look and it is once more the solid wooden door.

She told me after the journey:

> While I have been meditating and also jour-
> neying for the last fifteen years, I seldom
> have had such clear, connected images
> throughout the journey. This is also the first
> journey I have ever taken without a question
> in mind prior to the journey. I wonder if the
> removal of the pressure to "perform" (i.e. find
> an answer) allowed the "story" within the jour-
> ney to be experienced.
>
> As I descended the steps I was very aware of
> the voice of the guide. As she said the number
> of the steps to go down, her voice was crisp
> and commanding. As she talked between the
> steps, her voice was soft and reassuring — even
> coaxing. I believe that this combination of
> command and reassurance, would be very
> effective helping clients overcome resistance
> to journeys....
>
> As I remember the experience of the journey, I
> noticed a distinct difference in feeling between
> the early part, up until I saw the steps leading
> down into the water. The surprise at seeing the
> steps seemed to allow my intellect to turn off....
> There is a sense of peace and harmony that
> everything is all right. The garden is beautiful and
> peaceful and feels just right. It is bright, but not
> too bright; structured by plants being allowed to
> structure themselves. I do not wish to enforce
> my will on such a place (by pushing through
> the overgrown path), but have my will accepted

by politely asking. I have no trouble breathing under water. The tunnel is cool, but there is fresh air, and I have no difficulty finding my way.

There was a willingness, from the beginning, to look and experience all the journey had to offer.

At this point, the woman distinguishes the themes, patterns, and metaphors, embedded in her journey:
All three worlds of the shaman are represented:

1. the Lower (going down through water to the underworld),
2. the Middle (the garden), and
3. the Upper (flying out into space)

It is interesting to note here, that the three worlds may also be represented through the Greek temple, which Cirlot says, "symbolizes the intercommunication between the Three Worlds — the Lower, the Terrestrial, and the Upper" (1971:335).

She goes on to reflect,

The old woman...turns into a crow (crone), represents ancient-wisdom with her white hair and old-fashioned dress.

The most obvious theme in the journey is the recurring symbols of femininity: the entry room is round; has soft, plush, velvet-couches; is curved; with deep magenta colors; has an arched ceiling and an arched doorway leading out.

The pool of water is round and in a round clearing; the maze-like tunnels are curved; and the room in the castle is round. There is a woman who teaches, dressed in a soft, long dark dress. The images in space are curved.

Another theme is spirituality. In the entry room, both the ceiling and the door leading further into the unconscious are arched, as is often seen in temples. The room appears to be divided into thirds, three being the number of spirituality. The exterior building is a Greek temple and blindingly white. On return, the ceiling is a brilliant blue, which Gaskell says is the "symbol of the celestial regions...[or] the Kingdom of Heaven" (1981:773).

The underlying theme, most significant for me is concerned with structure and pattern. The first room appears very structured by being evenly divided between couches and open spaces. Out the window I can see the structure of stars in space. Outside, the garden is apparently growing wild, but the plants structured themselves. The clearing with the pool follows a similar structure as the entry room (if a perpendicular path were drawn through the pool and clearing, one could see two semicircles).

Around the pool and lining of the tunnel walls are stone patterns which hold the water and the openings within the tunnels. The underground tunnels, or mazes, also have a pattern which

I had no trouble tracing, although I did not consciously know that I was doing it.

Cirlot discusses labyrinths or mazes as being part of initiatory temples and says that tracing the labyrinth was "an initiation into sanctity, immortality and absolute reality" (1971:174-175).

The next pattern is that of the castle. Cirlot gives the metaphor that "a castle in the path of a wanderer is like the sudden awareness of a spiritual pattern" (1971:39). At this point in the journey, the structure and patterns start to shift. First, the old woman shifts her pattern and becomes a crow. To Native Americans, the crow itself is known as a shape shifter that can bend the laws of the physical universe.

> Then the old woman and I go out into space and the bright-sunlight shifts to darkness. In space we shift some pattern where I am apparently learning to shift dimensions by learning to "turn sideways."

If Cirlot is correct that "time is usually symbolized by a sheen as of shot silk" (1971:54), the shimmering blackness of space may also represent another dimension and another shift in pattern.

> I evidently do learn to do something because when we started to return I am able to shift my pattern into that of a crow.

> Back in the castle, the old woman tries to explain the pattern, but there is no pattern in her speech for me to understand. I can see the

two patterns, the underground maze and the out-in-space maze overlaying each other, but I cannot understand what I see.

As I leave the castle, I recognize that there must have been some shift in the pattern of the connection between the castle and the maze since I originally went down into the maze from the pool, but just entered the castle (which is on a higher physical plane than the pool) without going back up any steps. Therefore, on the way to the castle I am unaware of the patterns. On the way back out of the castle I am aware that there is not only a pattern, but the pattern has to shift to allow me to change levels between the maze and the castle without going up or down.

The journey left me with one image not interpreted. Why was the water so cold? And why was I told on the way out "not now" when I wanted another drink?

There are Celtic stories in which, after death, a stone brings forth water, one drink of which brings remembrance, and the second drink forgetfulness. That would have resulted in being told not to drink the second time, the implication being that it might be all right to drink later. Perhaps the interpretation of the water drinking scene might also indicate my final understanding as to what the journey was telling me.

There were many metaphors of understanding given in the journey, including the path "becoming clear;" I "come to a clearing;" I "have no difficulty finding my way;" and going straight into space "as a crow flies."

However, in the end, the understanding of what I was to do with the images escaped me. Both in being able to completely learn what the old woman was trying to teach me in space and in understanding what she was trying to tell me with the vision of the maze under the ground superimposed on the one out in space.

While a case might be made for the journey being an initiation into the ways of learning how to bring the spiritual and the unconscious together into consciousness using the image of the underground maze (the unconscious) transparent and overlaying the space maze, no other elements in the journey appear to support it. Another possibility might be to bring the unconscious and the rational together, as in drinking the water (the unconscious) at the pool from the rational right hand into the body on the Middle Level.

After the journey I was left, with a deep feeling of peace. Due to that feeling, there is less concern now about not understanding the message of the journey immediately. As with dreams that are not clear until months or sometimes years later, I can only expect that this remarkable journey will complete its message to me at a later time.

Nothing more needs to be said. She received a clear message and was able to talk about it. Her full understanding of the journey will grow with time.

What is important is that we keep moving, in the dance.

Are these experiences culture-specific? The answer is "no." Like archetypes, images emerge culturally conditioned, but the experience itself rises from a deeper universal level.

* * *

CASE NINE

In July 1992, a Russian professor of psychology at Moscow University wrote after her first drumming session:

> The first room was big and comfortable. The walls were soft (as if covered with some long woolen threads or fur of some animal). The room accepted me, calmed me down, and warmed me up.

> It was full of serenity and peace, but this peace was blended with mystery, sounds like some powerful music of the universe.

> The second room was much smaller, it was also soft and comfortable but my feelings were even stronger. They were the feelings of Mystery and Meaningfulness.

> I began to wait for something to emerge. Some time passed — and then a giant snake started crawling up from a far corner of the room.

It was big and powerful. Some great energy and power were felt in all of its movements. My first feeling was: "Now it is going to squeeze and strangle me as if i were a little mouse. It is quite obvious that in comparison to it I am nothing."

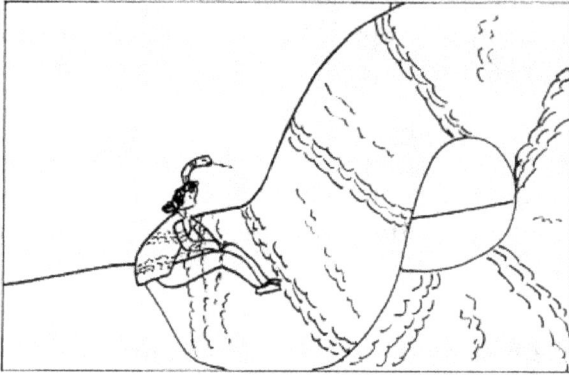

This giant snake kept approaching me, as if some energy were flooding the room. The room was too narrow for it and there was no place to hide. I felt neither fear nor despair. I was absolutely calm. "Is there any way out?" I thought. This question became the way of some inner resistance and the energy of this resistance was almost as strong as the energy of the approaching rings of the snake. Still, it was quite obvious that the snake would surely strangle me.

Suddenly I noticed that the small head of the snake started coming out of the crown of my head. I saw that it was very small. It kept moving up. I felt that the snake was crawling through me, flooding my body. I felt it moving, in my legs, belly, arms, breast, and head. Its body filled my body; it was very powerful, strong, and big.

Then, I turned into a stone. The color of the stone was light green, as if it were a semi-precious stone, usually found in necklaces. And again there arose a question, "What to do?" It was rather pleasant to be a stone, but it was not my choice. I just didn't want to be a stone. I felt neither panic nor tension, but I wanted to find a way out.

Then I noticed, to my surprise, that I was no longer a stone, I was ice. The transparent light green color was the color of ice on which the rays of the sun were falling.

The experience of myself started to change. The feeling of heaviness and being a stone dissolved, I became lighter. I was relieved; I now had a way out. The sun started melting me and I became a light blue cloud, floating up, higher and higher. I felt free and blissful.

At this very moment, I heard a voice, "You must come back into the room." I felt at a loss. I didn't know how I possibly could come down again, being so light and evaporated. That was absolutely impossible. But then I started to become a big drop of water, concentrated myself and came down into the comfortable room.

When I went up the stairs and opened my eyes, I was surprised by the feeling of freshness and inner clarity. There was that pervading sense of great mystery in everything around me.

This vision was experienced in Russia before the 1992 coup. The tension was palpable when we walked among stoic looking people on the streets. There was uncertainty, fear, hopelessness, and lack of orientation. The stages of transformation and the richness of her first journey into the less conscious regions of her mind heralded the arising of clarity, hope, and renewed strength. I don't want to interpret her experience further because, as I said before, the meaning of such transformations is the personal property of the visionary.

In July 1993, I conducted a series of workshops at the Psychology Department of the University of Vilnius, Lithuania. The students were young women in their early or late twenties. All embarked on the "journey" for the first time. The following accounts are unedited translations from Lithuanian into English. My interpreter and I checked the translations with the visionaries.

CASE TEN
One student reported her first Journey:

To find the first door which was big and made out of wood was easy. The first room was half dark. My eyes had to get used to the darkness. It was not a big room, more like a corridor. At the other end of the room I saw a metal door, nice looking but somewhat colder. There was no furniture in the room, it was empty. Despite a few windows it still was rather dark.

I went to the other room and was surprised by its yellow color. It was a big, golden room with ornaments. Later I saw more rooms and went into them. I looked at the pictures on the wall but they were not very interesting. Going from one room into the other, I felt there was nothing to do.

Then I decided to play, using my body. While I was somersaulting and jumping, I saw a dusty picture on the floor. I tried to clean the dust from the lower left corner and saw a very intense purple color. It was so intense that I became very excited and wanted to cry.

While I was sweeping away more dust, I saw a knight with a pike of the same color. Then, out of the color, a dragon appeared. I felt power but it was time to go back.

When I re-entered the room, it looked brighter, lighter. Before I left the room, to climb up the stairs again, I saw a blue pillow and other blue things.

During the journey, she became playful. Obviously she was now ready to trust the process. She experienced power, but first had to sweep away the "dust."

Let's look at her second journey on the next day:

I easily reached the first door. Sometimes I was faster than your words and needed to wait. When I entered the room, I was surprised that it was no longer dark. The only thing in the room was an old, rather ordinary bench. The whole room looked like a waiting hall.

When I opened the second door, there was nothing but space. I felt like I was losing control but moved into this space. In the right corner, I saw a garden slowly appearing. It was an orchard with big, red, juicy apples. I cannot remember whether I tried to eat some, but I remember that I thought about what I was supposed to do.

The garden looked like a sentimental picture. I remembered a wish I had in my childhood. I always wanted to lie on a cloud. So I did it now. The cloud was soft and it felt good. It was also a little bit frightening.

I felt something in my mouth and returned slowly. The first room was now bigger and there were two colors: white and blue. I liked this room much better.

She became more familiar with "traveling" and allowed childhood memories to manifest. She discovered that she could lie on clouds, but still had to work through some anxieties.

Here is the report of her third journey on the third day:

I went down the same steps, through the same first door. Everything was similar, but the room was now larger and brighter than in previous journeys and had some furniture. I was curious what would be behind the second door.

I opened the door and entered the very clouded space. I couldn't see anything and understood that I needed to wait. I felt lonely but then I saw something very big moving slowly toward me. It was a dragon. I could see his back. It was not dangerous, so I stayed calm. I just observed how he rose and started moving through the space, without any haste.

I became suddenly bored and asked him, "What do you need to do?" He said he wanted to fly and I helped him to find wings. There were the wings of Ikaros which did not work. Later on I thought that the best way would be to fly on the cloud. I showed him some clouds on which he could fly and he did.

I took the wings of Ikaros and was flying, too. In the center of the land appeared a fire and I went near it. The land was moving and little dragons were rising. They looked not too friendly. I was a little bit afraid and asked them, "What

do you need to feel better?" They said, "We
need sun light." I tried to concentrate on the
drum to send the clouds away. Then I saw the
sun. It was pleasant.

It was also time to return. When I came to the
first room, it looked the same but on the floor
was a big, soft carpet which made the room look
warmer.

She was showing others how to fly and helped to bring
out the sun. Her journeys reflect a progression of her cau-
tious explorations which she is now continuing on her own.

Though we had discussed neither mythology nor any
mythological symbolism in any workshop, images of
dragons appeared in many journeys.

❀ ❀ ❀

CASE ELEVEN

The second Lithuanian woman had the following experiences during her first journey:

the first door reminded me of my childhood
home. It opened to a room similar to the room
I lived in as a child, but there was no furniture.
There were many windows and flowers on the
wall. The pure light from the windows was
reflected on the floor.

The second door led to the next room and
again resembled the door of my bedroom at
home. I couldn't remember how the furniture was placed, but saw two beds pushed
together where my sister and I would sleep.
The beds occupied the largest part of the

room. Something transparent, grayish-black was flying over the beds. Maybe it was only a color spot; maybe it was something transparent and light. I was a little bit afraid, because it looked dangerous.

However, I used my breath and drew a curtain around it. The flying object changed color and seemed not to be so fearful anymore. Then I saw myself dancing. I was transparent and all things in the room were also. There was not enough space to move and not enough fresh air.

I began flying over the beds, and my transparent body changed its form. I was just movement and color. I felt the narrowness and closeness and looked for space and freshness. Then, suddenly, soundly and forcefully, the windows were opening and a strong fresh wind blew in.

Sometimes, I did not have any distinct form, but kept changing colors. I moved very fast and flew out into the low clouds. I saw a forest and low white clouds. Then the drum stopped playing and I saw very bright sun light.

She did not report on her second journey. On her third journey,

the ten steps led to an ancient Greek amphitheater. When I was standing on the last, the tenth step, I saw the door and the room were under water and I could not see the walls of the room. In the water it was difficult to see anything. Water plants were swaying and I began to move smoothly.

The second door led into a big field. Naked people were dancing in a circle around a big fire. Their movements were very beautiful, strong, and perfect. I saw myself dancing in the center of the circle near the fire.

At one time, my body rose up and I was dancing above the ground. Then the ground split and disappeared. I felt the movement but could not see. The feeling was associated with wholeness and freedom.

When the drum stopped playing, I quickly went back to the amphitheater and felt a little bit ashamed about my ecstatic dancing.

At the time of the workshop, the Russian Army was leaving Lithuania after over fifty years of occupation. When I walked through the city, the feeling of relief was enlivening everything. Though there were still some ruins — buildings and walls which had been destroyed during World War II, quite a few medieval buildings had remained intact. The old university in the center with its colorful wall paintings, the churches, and the pilgrimage center above an old gateway, were filled with people. A dark shadow was lifting. Who would doubt that there was reason to dance again, ecstatically?

✣ ✣ ✣

Case Twelve

The third Lithuanian woman told me that, during her first journey, she went down with great expectations. The first room was a bedroom. I heard the drum and had to leave the room. There was no message.

Through the windows of the second room I saw a city with skyscrapers. I was in a hurry but saw something in writing on a table. I told myself, "Don't forget it; write it down". It said, "You need to do your job."

During her second journey, she saw a six-year-old child standing nearby.

I asked the child, "Why are you here?" And the child said, "I feel pity for you." The child pitied many people. It was sad and bewildered and also angry.

I grew up angry but later was able to express myself better and knew how to nourish myself: "Be good to yourself." I could not express it when I was a child. At that time, I felt a lack of warmth and understanding. I was the oldest child of four brothers and sisters.

When she stepped out through the second door during the third journey, she saw a tall tower of a castle.

I knew there was a second tower but it was covered by clouds. It started raining and the rain reminded me of tears. The clouds were crying and then dissolved.

Then the second tower emerged and the castle

turned into a tunnel. I moved through it very fast. It was dark with bright lights on the walls. Suddenly the tunnel turned into a river which flowed into another, bigger river.

I was on a ship and kept moving. Then I needed to return. When I entered the first room again, I met a very special friend. We were leaving the room together and went up to the fifth step. Then I understood I needed to go alone but I carry him in my heart.

Her responsibilities were no longer a heavy load. She had found nourishment on her own, even though her special friend was no longer with her.

❦ ❦ ❦

CASE THIRTEEN
The fourth Lithuanian woman said,

During my first journey, I saw steep cement stairs and the steps were dirty. Downstairs was an ancient iron door. I knew how to open the door and entered the room. It was twilight and I could see the dirty floor and the stone walls, with cobwebs in the corners. Later I saw a joiner's table with some tools on it.

The next door was an old wooden door. When I opened it, I saw a big gray room. The hall looked empty and cold. I couldn't understand what kind of place it was. Suddenly I discovered small pictures on the walls. It was a show room. I couldn't see the pictures clearly even when I tried to go closer. Then I felt tired and looked around. I wanted to find a chair and saw a row of them in a niche. I sat down and saw that the walls were made out of white glazed bricks.

There was a corridor or a narrow room in front of me and I understood that it was an operating room in a hospital. I didn't see any person but I saw lights. And then I noticed a bed on wheels in the middle of the room. I couldn't see whether somebody was lying in the bed, because the bed was behind a screen.

Suddenly (with the sound of the bowl), I went through the door on the side. Going straight ahead, I came to another room. This room was dark and the floor was made from black polished granite. The room was empty and I was afraid to enter. I was waiting for somebody, but nobody came.

Then I had to go back. I felt anxiety because I was a great distance away from the first room. I had to run because I wanted to reach the first room in time. I didn't see anything on my way. I left the first room very quickly, closed the door and went up the stairs very easily.

She did not report on her second journey. On her third journey,

the stairs were very ordinary and I saw a bright wooden door. When I opened the door, I noticed a bright empty room with big windows. The only dark thing in this room was the next door.

Then I opened the second door and saw a gallery. I could see a high ceiling and columns on the sides. A row of black men entered the gallery. They were wearing distinctly dark clothes. They began to dance in a circle in the middle of the gallery to the sound of the drum. Their movement quickened, their circle became smaller and smaller. They looked like a gray spiral. Then the spiral began to rise and disappeared.

I could see a park around the gallery. The trees were tall and green, and the weather was fine. I wanted to walk and suddenly noticed myself being in a small train which went through the park.

Then I began to feel that I was on a ship sailing on a river. I saw seagulls flying behind our ship. I tossed bits of bread to them.

Then I saw a mountain at the shore. I felt that I was on top of that mountain and fog was rising. I saw a fire and watched it until I fell asleep. I woke up in the meadow near the small cemetery in the country, where my mother is buried. I was lying on the grass. It was sunnier and I felt an energy coming from the grass and the ground. I felt the energy and strength entering me. The power pulled me up and I flew to the top of an oak tree in front of me. I became part of it. My oak tree was growing in the park.

Then I had to go back. I flew or jumped down, found, opened, then closed the second door behind me, crossed the room and left by the first door. I was tired and it was difficult for me to climb up.

She connected with the Source of her strength and is on the way of becoming more efficient in utilizing this infinite energy.

The following seven reports were written down at a sea resort outside of Talinn (capital of Estonia) on the Baltic Sea. The women, mostly psychologists and health practitioners, were between thirty to forty years of age. The reports were written in Estonian and translated by my interpreter together with each woman.

✧ ✧ ✧

CASE FOURTEEN

She did not indicate on which of the three journeys she was reporting:

> I was descending a strong staircase. It was dark, moist, and covered with moss. The first door was a massive iron door with a huge metal ring for pulling. There were some people in the room. They had been emotionally very significant for me in the past but I treated them like strangers.
>
> The other door was a wooden door with beautiful engravings. There was no room behind it, only open space. It was dark. There were only different colors and geometrical structures in front of me. I felt lonely and sad.
>
> It was the space of God. There were no illusions any more; the reality was basic and awesome. I did not feel safe but I knew that I had no choice. It was my fate.
>
> When I returned to the room, there were no people anymore. The staircase was covered with red cloth and it was lighted.

She had begun to distance herself from the past. Having resigned herself to her "fate," she found the upward staircase covered with red cloth and there was light.

✧ ✧ ✧

CASE FIFTEEN

I only got a report on this woman's third journey:

I was moving down the stairs very quickly. It took really only a moment to go down and pass through the two doors. I didn't have time to see what kind of doors they were. I didn't have time to look at the first room either.

I went very quickly to the second room. It was long, very long, turning a little bit to the right. I mean it didn't have straight walls. I couldn't see the end of the room because it was turning to the right. The wall on the left resembled something like an architect's drawing. In the left corner of the room, in front of the bright wall which resembled a drawing, there was space or a room which opened downward. It was very deep. Gray-blue in color, it was full of metal structures. I was standing and looking down and felt that there may be two different ways for me.

I looked at the bright wall and felt something drawing me into this bright endless somewhere. The room was changing and looked now like a long bright tube. At the same time there was, to the left, gray-blue immense emptiness full of metal which would lead me down.

When we finished, I felt that my hands were very heavy. I couldn't move them (and I didn't want to do so). However, it was a very pleasant feeling.

She had started to work through obstructions and was trying to clear her sight. It is interesting that in many of these reports long bright tubes or tunnels appear (similar to those reported by individuals who go through Out-Of-Body or Near-Death experiences). Metal structures seem to represent obstacles.

⚜ ⚜ ⚜

Case Sixteen

She reported on her first journey,

> As I was the translator, I could not see the steps very clearly. The first door was old and made of wood. So was the second.

> Behind the second door, I saw a great fire burning and somebody around it. There was drumming around the fire. Through the flames, I saw a face. The face was unknown to me. Somebody was suffering. Then I recognized that it belonged to my friend. He was wearing richly decorated costume and a red-blue cap on his head. Then I saw the face of my grandfather through the flames. He had been dead for 22 years. I asked him how to help my friend who is in trouble but I couldn't get an answer. The sound of the bowl called me back.

During the second journey,

> as I was translating, I could not see the steps and the doors very clearly. I jumped right in, being in a hurry, like not wanting to miss a train.

> When the bowl began to sound, I started to slide. There was some fog around my feet. Then

I saw the earth from above, like from an air-
plane — the mountains, the rivers, etc.

Suddenly I was tied with my back to a wooden
cross. The cross was placed on a huge flagstaff
and was going round and round and my head
became very dizzy. Then I saw the flag in front
of me – white background with green and pink
and lots of symbols. There was a dark symbol
I remember especially well. The symbol was
unknown to me. At present, it is not possible
for me to guess its meaning.

After the journey, I felt extremely bad for many
hours. I felt faint and had a terrible headache.
The situation cleared up during the next day's
meditation.

During her third journey,

red steps were taking me down. I was in front
of an old and heavy wooden door. It had a

nice smell. The room had wooden walls. It was empty but there was a pleasant smell like smoke. The second door had a metal handle like in everyday life.

Then I was in space, with some clouds around my feet. I started running on a huge tambourine to the rhythm of the drum.

Suddenly I became aware of a physical problem. The energy in my neck was blocked. I felt like a piece of meat on the tambourine, pounded by a large hammer. I had a sensation of increased vibrations in the neck region but the sensations were very pleasant.

Finally, I saw myself rising totally refreshed and very light. I felt relief. My neck was much better than before.

She had been disadvantaged by having to translate the induction but managed to "jump in." In addition, she had to work through her physical and emotional difficulties. Therefore, the message, which came up during her first journey, was not fully revealed.

✤ ✤ ✤

CASE SEVENTEEN

During the first and second journey, she was too tired to remember. On her third journey, she reported.

The stairway was easy. I was awake all the time. What was I doing?

The first door was big, brown, and covered with metal ornaments. It was difficult to open. The room was large and looked like a church in Uppsala, with columns and a cupola. I looked around in the room and thought that, for some reason, the first room should not be so big. I tried to make it smaller which took a lot of energy. Now it was too small, but I wanted to make it round, because sound and spirit wanted to fly.

I found myself at the entrance to a larger church. My mind was flying easily. I was very light. It felt good to be weightless, though my body was still there. I wanted to be under the cupola in the middle of the church. Light was falling down and I received some spiritual energy.

Then I had to go through the second door, which was at the end of the hall behind a sarcophagus. It was small, white and covered with gold ornaments.

The room behind it was even smaller and dark. At first, I couldn't see anything, no walls. The floor and the ceiling were made from black marble. On the right side of the cupola was a wall, in the front and on the left side it had a zigzag line. I went into the small room.

There was a hole in the ceiling. My soul or my spirit ascended, like going through a long tunnel very quickly. I flew up. At the end, my spirit exploded in different colors and became a fountain of light.

After some time, my spirit slowly descended. I wanted to stay but had to return. Around the hole in the floor was a mandala I had the opportunity to ask what was waiting for me in the future and a pearl jumped up. This ornament knew the answer but I found I should first ask myself, "What is the meaning of this symbol?"

The return trip was very easy and natural.

She had a liberating experience and is now working on the symbols she saw.

❀ ❀ ❀

CASE EIGHTEEN
During the first journey, for her

going down was not difficult. The door to the first room was wooden, heavy, and old. The first room itself was dome-shaped, with a circular floor and dark stone walls, without any windows, no furniture, in half-light. No one was there.

The door to the second room was also wooden, heavy, and old. The second room was big, high and reminded me of a sacred building. There were many windows and colorful light but no furniture and no other beings.

When the drum beat became stronger, I suddenly felt that I was circling around the middle of the room like the Islamic Sufis do. I could see a figure, but only for a single moment. It flashed, from the backside — possibly a man. I began to sense that I was circling around a living fire and I asked, "What am I doing here?" A voice answered, "You are cleansing yourself." I asked, "From what?" The answer was, "From excessive thinking."

Then a white-clad women appeared and went through the full length of the room before they disappeared. As they were going past me, I had a good and light feeling.

The journey ended with the sound of the Tibetan bowl.

During her second journey,

the first door and room were similar to the first journey, but there were now windows.

When I entered the second room, there were ruins of a building, surrounded by spacious nature. I pushed the strong flow forward from my chest and began to move further with this flow.

When the drum speeded up, a tunnel appeared around me. At the end of the tunnel, I saw a dark cosmic panorama with many little lights. The flight lasted quite a long time, and I began to come closer to the greater sources of light. At last, I entered into one of them.

Suddenly a man's figure with long white hair appeared. I asked, "Who are you? Are you my guardian angel, inner pilot, my deeper nature, or something like that?" (To my mind these are all the same.) But there was no answer and the figure dissolved. Flying further, more and more beings appeared. They were powerful and non-material.

Then the drumming stopped and my journey was interrupted like the first one.

During her third journey,

the door and the room were the same as in the first and second journey.

Rain was falling; a black liquid came gently down. I began to see a sailing boat in the distance. I had to wait a long time for the boat to come to the beach. Somebody put a smaller boat into the water. The blue sky got darker. A man appeared in the sky and disappeared quickly. Nobody was in the boat but there were dried maple leaves at its bottom. (Maple is the astrological tree which makes you stronger.) More maple leaves kept falling into the boat.

I stepped into the boat and moved slowly toward the sailing boat. I climbed the ladder and stepped into the boat. There was nobody there. When I walked to the front part of the sail boat, I met several sailors. They were very pleasant men, with gray beards. I asked them what route to choose, and one showed me the route, it led toward the setting sun. It was like a highway toward the sun.

I started to sail. The sea was quiet and I felt gentle waves, falling and rising, like our life.

The journey was interrupted because the drum stopped.

She moved toward the area worthwhile of further explorations and had begun to pave her "highway toward the sun."

* * *

Case Nineteen

She reported on her first journey:

The steps were half-lit. They were made out of

concrete or stone. The first door was old and wooden, with iron ornaments.

The first room was old-fashioned red. I was surprised that there was a TV. At first there was no second door but I thought, "It must be there," and then I found a dark spot in front of me. I thought it must be the door. Finally the door appeared.

Only then could I go through the second door. There was darkness. I used the sound of drum to make light and there appeared a large valley and a river.

Part of the sky was bright but I wanted to see more. I found that I was in a green forest, wandering on a narrow road.

Then I saw an eagle in the sky. I felt connected with him, like I was flying next to him. I went further on the narrow road, then flew up and saw the road from the sky.

Then I went back to the first room which had not changed, neither had the steps.

She began to use sound "to make light" and learned that she could fly.

※ ※ ※

CASE TWENTY
During her first journey, she

could see the steps very clearly. At the beginning, they were in the dark but as I was going down, they became lighter.

The first door, made out of wood, was very simple.

The first room was very long, like a corridor. It was made out of stone, like a monastery or church. On the left, there were small windows and light was falling down from them. There was a lot of dust. At the very end of the room, there was a chair. At first, it seemed that somebody was sitting on it but when I came closer, I realized nobody was there.

The second door was made out of hardwood. It was a double door, one half opened to one side, the other to the other side.

The second room was in red and black. In the center of the room was a table with chairs around it. At the end of the room, I saw a red throne. I was waiting for some time. When I began to approach the table, rays formed a light road and I was moving on this road faster and faster. There were some turns. It was as if I were in a tunnel. After one turn, to the left side, there was more space and it was light. I stopped. I needn't to go further. Then I found steps which were going up. They were circular.

Something was coming down these steps. It was a shining snake. The snake wound around a pole, head down. I saw him above me and I didn't want to go up.

I went back to the first room which looked familiar. The steps were straight.

During her second journey,

the steps were similar to the steps in the first journey. The room was also the same but darker. The second door was dark and had double panels, as in the first journey.

The second room was dark when I entered. The ceiling appeared in dark blue color, like in a Gothic church. I felt like lying on the floor and looking up.

Then I thought I was in Notre Dame in Paris. White clouds appeared and I seemed to be lying on the clouds or on sand (in a desert). Then I saw you. You were going from the right to the left side. After a while you transformed into a bird. I asked you, "What can you tell me"? But you said nothing.

Then I heard you asking me to go back. Nothing had changed, only the steps were higher.

The images of "tunnels," "lying on clouds" and "flying" indicate movement toward liberation.

In conclusion, it should be noted that all twenty cases recounted, have indeed, been collected from women. The first reason for this is that the grant to write this book had been given to foster the creativity of women. The second, among many other reasons, was that I found women more willing than men to explore their being. Women were also more willing to talk about their inner processes. On the other hand, there is no reason that anyone, regardless of race and gender, cannot search for the Source. I collected equally meaningful stories from men.

It is interesting to note that one recurring image in many participants descriptions was the dragon, an ancient symbol found in all cultures. In Chinese folklore, for example, it is said when carps swim down the river, upon reaching the sea, they will become dragons; and the martial arts speak of the "dragon rising from the sea." In one of the cases mentioned, the dragon was perceived as male because the journeyer was a woman, looking for a complement to her femininity. In several cases, the dragon appeared as the most potent symbol for transformation.

This book, however, has not been written to offer easy symbolic interpretations. My purpose was to invite exploration. On the spiritual level, we are all the same, but on the material level we are not. When archetypes rise from the unconscious level, they become culturally, as well as, individually conditioned. We need the ego to become creative. However, after it has fulfilled its purpose, our ego should merge, once again, with the Source.

❦ ❦ ❦

Why do we forget that increasing awareness is a life-long process? Why do we forget that we will be ultimately rewarded? The all-sustaining Source is infinite, timeless, and, in fact, available all the time; not only when a need arises. We can see the Light in the Dark and carry it with us wherever we go.

In the next chapter, I will talk about other doors of perception.

III. Methods and Practices

Doors to Perception

The aspects that are most important for us are hidden
because of their simplicity and familiarity.
One is unable to notice something because
it is always before one's eyes.

Wittgenstein (1953:50)

After you decide to use a door of perception, it is good practice to center yourself by bringing your conscious attention to your mind and body.

Focus Exercise and Breath Work

Begin with a few exercises to relax your body. There is, for example, a Qi-gong exercise where you stand erect, with slightly bent knees, loose in your shoulders and arms. Then start shaking your whole body, first, slowly but then accelerating until you shake as fast as you can. Feel the "cobwebs" falling to the floor! When your jaws start making small sounds, it proves that you are loosening up. After three minutes, slowly decrease the speed of shaking until you come to a stand-still. It is important to remain standing for a few minutes. The stillness allows the experience to sink in and you can enjoy the energy rushing throughout your body.

Then, clear your mind by breathing naturally but consciously, at your own pace, sending away negative feelings and thoughts with the out breath. Really sweep your entire body from top to bottom with your breathing. Enjoy the release of the used air and the nourishment of the incoming air throughout your body. Keep up conscious breathing for at least five minutes before you approach any of the following doors.

CONTEMPLATION

Look for a comfortable, secluded place. At home, you may want to sit near a window which looks out into nature. In nature, you may want to lie in a meadow, lean against a tree, or sit on a rock and contemplate on a sunrise or a sunset.

1. If your feeling functions are predominant, you will experience awe and appreciate the beauty of this daily event.
2. If your sensation functions are predominant, you will enjoy the colors and shapes of clouds and the brilliancy of light.
3. If your thinking functions are predominant, you will be reminded of the relationship of the earth to the sun and of the position of the sun in the galaxy, contemplating on the clockwork of the universe.
4. If your intuitive functions are predominant, you will ponder about the miraculous rising of the light and its significance.

Jung used these four functions to explain how differently each of us experiences similar events (1960:145-146, 1971). Why don't we realize that, each time we perceive a "daily" event, we experience it differently? Everything is in flux and we, as well as, the circumstances, ever so subtly, keep changing. You can also contemplate on:

1. the movements of a cloud,
2. the flight of a bird,
3. the flow of a river or the descent of a waterfall,
4. the waves of an ocean,
5. the beauty of a flower,

6. the flame of a candle,
7. the picture of a loved one or
8. the picture of a landscape which holds special meaning for you.

You contemplate on the object you selected until you have fully absorbed its nature and have become the object. Notice how it feels. Notice its colors, its sounds, its fragrances or smells. What taste do you experience on your tongue? How does it touch your skin?

According to Deikman,

> Contemplation is, ideally, a non-analytic apprehension—non-analytic because discursive thought is banished and the attempt is made to empty the mind of everything except the precept of the object...Cognition is inhibited in favor of perception [that means] the active intellectual style is replaced by a receptive perceptual mode. (1996:27-31)

If possible, devote at least half an hour each day to contemplation; preferably, at the same hour (early in the morning or late at night). Each day is a new day.

MEDITATION

Select a form of meditation provided by your belief system. If you cannot decide, I want to introduce you to Insight (Vipassana) Meditation which is taught by Theravada monks in Southeast Asia (Thailand, Burma, Laos, Cambodia, and Sri Lanka). It is the earliest form of Buddhist meditation.

I suggest Insight Meditation because it does not require belief in any dogma and it is, indeed, the simplest and most effective way to increase awareness. It improves concentration and helps refine your capacity to perceive.

If there are no Buddhist monasteries offering meditation instruction in your neighborhood, you can look for a quiet place in nature or select a corner in your apartment which you will use exclusively for meditation. You may want to light a candle, or burn incense, and set some flowers out to purify and honor the place you have selected. Though it is not absolutely necessary, you may want to prepare an altar by putting a sacred object next to the flowers and the candle.

Then sit down, either cross-legged or, if this is too difficult, you can use a chair. It is important to be comfortable. When you sit on a chair, your feet should be slightly apart and your back should be kept straight at all times (this is the most comfortable position to maintain concentration for at least twenty minutes). Your hands should rest on your knees; or you can select the traditional meditation position by putting one hand over the other, with the palms up and the thumbs slightly touching. During meditation, you can occasionally look at your thumbs. When they are slightly touching, your concentration is good. When they have drifted apart, you are too relaxed and, when they are pressed against each other, you are too tense.

Breathe normally, in through the nose and out through the mouth. When no thoughts arise, just contemplate the rising and falling of your breath. Be aware of your whole body. Awareness of your entire being is important.

Deikman, tells us,

> the active phase of contemplative meditation is a preliminary to the stage of full contemplation, in which the subject is caught up and absorbed in a process he initiated but which now seems autonomous, requiring no effort. Instead, passivity — self-surrender — is called for, an open receptivity amidst the "darkness" resulting from the banishment of thoughts and sensations and the renunciation of goals and desires directed toward the world (1969:29)

Insight meditation is practiced in three parts: two steps to clear your mind before you begin to observe what is going on in your mind (i.e., practicing forgiveness and loving kindness); and the third is to remain aware of your body and breath.

To begin practicing forgiveness, recite the following verses aloud, and really mean what you say.

If by deed, speech or thought,
I have foolishly done wrong,
May all forgive me, honored ones,
Who are in wisdom and compassion strong.
I freely forgive anyone
Who may have hurt or injured me.

I freely forgive myself.
Sending loving kindness to everyone:

Now, mentally repeat the following verses and, with each line, send loving kindness to the person(s) mentioned, one by one. Give yourself enough time to do so. In this case, begin with yourself.

May I be well, happy, and peaceful!
May my teachers be well, happy, and peaceful!
May my parents be well, happy, and peaceful!
May my relatives be well, happy, and peaceful!
May my friends be well, happy, and peaceful!
May the indifferent persons be well, happy, and peaceful!
May the unfriendly persons be well, happy, and peaceful!
May all meditators be well, happy, and peaceful!
May all beings be well, happy, and peaceful!

Then recite the following verse:

May suffering ones be suffering free and the fear struck
fearless be!
May the grieving shed all grief, and all beings find relief!

Then during the third and main part of meditation, while sitting quietly for twenty minutes, remain aware of your body and your breath. Keep your back straight (perhaps, moving slightly, leaning back and forth when you experience some pain). And check your thumbs to find out whether you are maintaining the right concentration.

Meditation teachers tell, at this point, a legend of the Buddha practicing austerities to the extreme, by eating only one kernel of rice each day. So that he would not die before enlightenment, the gods sent Indra to teach him the right concentration. Indra appeared with a lute whose strings were strung not too loosely and not too tightly, they were strung just right to produce the right tone, and the Buddha understood.

You can close your eyes. To prevent yourself from falling asleep, it is recommended to keep your eyes half open; looking approximately three feet ahead at the floor.

Throughout the meditation, watch your breath going in and out, *allowing only one thought at a time*. After you have explored the content of one thought, sensation, or feeling, go to the next one, until no thought, sensation, or feeling are left and you simply observe the going out and coming in of your breath. The goal is to develop one-pointedness of the mind. You want to increase awareness of your thoughts, feelings and sensations—in your body and your mind. Also note everything around you.

The beginning and end of the twenty-minute meditation can be indicated by sounding a Tibetan bowl. (To time yourself, you can put a clock in front of you.)

After the twenty-minute period, realize that you have accumulated merit. If your belief system allows it, you may want to share this merit by reciting the following verses:

> *May all beings share this merit which we have thus*
> *acquired for the acquisition of all kinds of happiness!*
> *May beings inhabiting heaven and earth, angels and*
> *others of mighty powers, share this merit of ours!*
> *May they long protect the Teachings!*

If you never have meditated before, you may want to start with ten minutes and sit longer when you are more familiar with this kind of meditation. Twenty minutes in the morning and before going to bed are sufficient to produce beneficial effects. Progress depends on the quality of your meditation.

It is important to write down your experience—difficulties and benefits—in your diary immediately after the session to establish a record of your spiritual development.

❦ ❦ ❦

Insight Meditation has been practiced for over 2,500 years. I did not see any need for changing the traditional words. Words are only the vehicle for a well-tested practice. Words build a safe structure so that a receptive attitude develops and your skills of being quiet and paying attention are refined (Maupin, 1969:1770).

Remember that you should not try to fight distractions, as Maupin explains,

> if you attempt to prevent distractions...you may get into unproductive blank states, or get distracted by the task of preventing distractions, or become tense. If you patiently return to the meditation, gradually your attention to the object will replace the distractions, and your physical relaxation will make it possible for the flow of thoughts to decrease.
>
> It is also important that you do not have some preconceived notion of what should happen in a "good" session....
>
> As the ego activity is reduced, inner material, some of it formerly outside awareness, begins to emerge (1969:181-182).

See also, Ven. U. Silananda (1990).

Dream Work

When using your dreams to explore less conscious regions of your mind, you learn to listen to yourself and become less dependent on others. If you have a choice to make between many alternatives, but do not have all the information to make the right decision, you can use the technique to search inside yourself for the answers:

Every night, before falling asleep, think of a question regarding a decision you have to make, and visualize all possible outcomes.

Deep inside of you, answers have been stored in your DNA and your different memory banks which have not reached your conscious levels yet.

There will be images which can neither be explained by wishful thinking, nor by being reflections of past events. There will be sensations which do not reflect what you have eaten and/or drunk during the last twenty-four hours. These "new" images are what you are looking for. You can work with them because they show you the other side of your "doors of perception."

To exemplify, I offer two stories from my own dream work.

When I am depressed, my dreams surprise me every time, by being powerful and joyful. My dreams obviously attempt to balance my state of mind and remind me of inner resources.

Once I had a career choice to make and could not decide which of four alternatives would be the best. (I simply did not have sufficient information to make a reasonable decision.) Therefore, shortly before falling asleep, I visualized all four alternatives as far as I could to foresee their consequences and asked my dream to come up with one answer. I got a clear answer, and, ret-rospectively, it turned out to be, indeed, the best choice I could have made.

What does science think about dreams? Freud, for example, suggested that

> Dream formation and early phases of the orga-nization of the dream will not be represented in the conscious experience of the dreamer. The typical condition of sleep is a state of uncon-sciousness, a state in which no mental activity is available to personal awareness or to report to others....

> The unconscious process which instigates dream formation is affective in character, and in partic-ular, it is some derivative of the primary motives of sex and destructive hostility....

In its final form, the dream is a distorted and sym-bolic rather than a manifest, direct expression of the impulses which instigate it....

> If repressed affect provides the energy for dream construction, perceptual-memorial events provide the raw material....

> The day residues...are the basic elements of the dream, but it would be misleading to conceive the dream as an orderly and logical sequence of such memories...being "worked over"...the ultimate dream product is a complicated and bizarre patterning of the original elements...it will be difficult to establish precisely what they

are....for purposes of dramatic representation... the repressed impulses may be successfully disguised [to evade censorship], so that the presentation will be as economical as possible....[Dream work includes] condensation, displacement and symbolization....[They] make the dream progressively less intelligible to waking consciousness and progressively detached from the moorings in unretouched sensory memory (in Foulkes, 1969:118-120).

Not as comprehensive or detailed as Freud, Adler then developed a theory which "formed a large part of the conceptual foundation of several recent and highly influential dream theories" (e.g., by Erich Fromm and Calvin Hall). Adler said that

Sleeping and waking thoughts are not totally incompatible...we must recognize the essential continuity of all forms of thought....

The instigation of dreams is not always...due to sexual or hostile motives, any more than waking thought (in Foulkes, 1969:121).

Like Freud, Adler felt that we dream when we are troubled by something. Ullman (1962:20) characterized the unresolved problems as "sore spots" which "press upon us during sleep." There seems to be a greater stress in Adler than in Freud...upon the expressive nature of symbolic representation. In dreaming we make use of those images and incidents which best agree with our style of life and which best express the present problem. This relatively strong emphasis on the symbol that expresses rather than the symbol which disguises is consistent with the notion of a continuity between waking and sleeping thought (Foulkes, 1969:121-122).

The continuity of thoughts not only from the waking to the sleeping state but also from the sleeping (less censored) state to the state of consensus reality became the topic for later research. For further information on dream work, I recommend Feinstein and Krippner (1988), Krippner and Dillard (1988), La Berge (1985) and Ullman and Zimmerman (1979).

Music

In the beginning was sound. Vibrations of the first sound set the universe in motion. Each cell of our body continues to respond to the vibrations coming from "inner space" and outer space."

You can explore which music you resonate with best, be it classical music, the sounds of a harpsichord, Japanese flute, or an impressionistic combination of instruments. You may want to look for music to:

1. soothe and heal,
2. encourage and inspire, and/or
3. transcend.

Like a medicine chest, you can keep a variety of music ready to treat your moods and imbalances.

You can also look for music which carries you into other dimensions, e.g., Mickey Hart's *Yamantaka* (Tibetan god who conquers *Yama* [death] and sublimates sensual desires). Hart leads you into outer space and you can ride the sounds to explore what is stored inside of you Also see Heinze (1992) and Campbell (1991, 1992).

✦ ✦ ✦

Sound has power, so have words. Therefore, you should also be aware of negative programming. Western physicians, for example, describe the course of an illness without leaving any hope or chance for possible change. Patients are hypnotized into following a degenerative pattern. You can, however, produce sounds to counteract negative programming and evoke the Source.

> You must...realize that what kills you is not so much the actual disease itself as it is your own

mind that is tempted to surrender to the disease. Take your mind and occupy it fully in a very exciting project or occupation. This will give the body time to heal itself. (Keeney, 1994:125).

DANCE

Music moves and invites us to dance. Music and dance activate your creative forces so that your body, mind, emotions and soul can merge. Indian ragas best express the "search of the soul for the Beloved" and the "Beloved" is God.

One transformative image is Shiva, an ascetic outcast among Indian gods, who is often depicted in the Dance of Creation and Destruction. He dances inside a circle of fire which consumes what is decaying or already dead. The snakes in his hair are blown by the Cosmic Wind. And, while he is sounding the skull drum (*damaru*), he subdues demons with his feet, so a new universe can emerge from the purified ground. You, too, can dance through all the phases of your renewal!

When a child has moved through the birth canal into a separate life, it still stays connected with the pulse of the universe. Movement is life. Breath sustains life. Dance regenerates energies which have fallen into disuse or have been abused. These energies can be re-awakened so that they continue to inform and to nourish life.

Keeney discovered in the gospels, one of the gnostic texts (the *Acts of John),* that Jesus assembled His disciples in Gethsemane prior to being arrested. He asked them "to form a circle, holding each other's hands, Himself standing in the middle." He then began a chant inviting them to dance, "He who does not dance does not know what happens." Keeney then cites a report on the Ghost Dance religion where

> Indians and white people were dancing to-
> gether...Jesus gathered with a large number of
> Indians and taught them a dance.... The Holy

father had said that it was time to renew the earth...
that the Indians and the white people were to be
one people and that he was available to everyone
in their spiritual vision (Keeney, 1994:66-67).

In the dance of Shiva, in the dance of the Christ of
the gnostic gospels, and in the Native American Indian
Ghost Dance, the dancers reconnect, gain wisdom, and
generate healing.

Swimming

Life emerges from water. You swam in the womb of your mother and, after having been born, long to re-experience this "oceanic feeling." Water conveys undifferentiated bliss. Swimming is, indeed, another form of meditation and the most direct way of experiencing deautomatization, unity, and "trans-sensate phenomena" (Deikman, 1969:41). When you surrender to the water, it opens its loving arms and caresses you. Trusting the water, you are carried by it.

Obviously, I am not talking about occasions where natural forces agitate large bodies of water. In such situations, you can still admire the interplay of wind and water and be invigorated by this sight. For swimming, however, it is advisable to select a calm river, lake or sea. If none of these are available in your neighborhood, an open-air swimming pool may be sufficient. (Avoid indoor pools because the smell of chlorinated water diminishes the joy of breathing.)

Swimming involves your whole body and is the quickest way to interconnect.

Vision Quest

In America, we are familiar with the vision quest of the Native American Indians. They go on a *hanblecheya*, to be alone in the wilderness, to fast and to pray. This is a culture-specific activity. However, Christians, Jews, and Muslims go into seclusion, to fast and pray for similar reasons. (Jesus, for example, went into the desert for forty days.)

Many of the world religions speak of vision quests; local folk religions never abandoned this tradition. The African American church in its early days, for example, was committed to individuals seeking a vision which was typically sought "by fasting and praying for three days in a swamp or isolated cemetery" (Keeney, 1994:58). Zora Neal Hurston

> interviewed several people who were initially unwilling to believe the visions they received and asked God for proof....

> A prayer fast in the wild was a form of spiritual practice for the early day African American church as well as in the earliest days of Christianity (Keeney, 1994:58).

IV. Epilogue

Bridges of Light

To be enlightened is to be aware, always,
of total reality in its immanent otherness
— to be aware of it and yet to remain
in a condition to survive as an animal,
to think and feel as a human being,
to resort whenever expedient to systematic reasoning.
Our goal is to discover
that we have always been
where we ought to be

Huxley (1963:78).

This book has been written to prevent and counteract alienation from the Source. I sincerely hope I succeeded and encouraged you to be inspired and nourished by the "Light."

Jill Puree has talked about the breathing cosmos and the "evolutionary spiral." She said that, in the early days of humanity, as in childhood, there was no separation between ourselves and the outside world, until we, individually...became self-conscious. As a result of successive windings, our individual and collective ego crystallized and we could see ourselves as subject, and as distinct from the world....the continuum differentiated into 'things.' Each branched into more things... until the continuum had developed into a hierarchical language, which once flowed in verbs and processes, broke up into nouns and connectives.

> [Another] stage for the individual is that of intuitive knowledge or enlightenment, in which subject and object again become one... In this spiral, every one of us all over the globe, is like a light becoming gradually brighter, until there are so many and are so intense, that there is one light; the light of cosmic consciousness, or what Teilhard de Chardin has called the 'psychical convergence of the universe upon itself: the Omega Point' (1974:9-10).

As soon as you recognize that you walk in darkness, you can select one of the doors which lead to heightened perception. You can be illuminated by the information and knowledge which is waiting for you.

You can contemplate and meditate. You can ask your dreams to bring up the light. You can listen to music. You can swim and you can dance yourself into the middle of the stream. You can go on a journey or a vision quest. And you can recall the ecstasy of past experiences which carried the Light of Knowing into the Dark.

> Only when people live in small villages can they care for one another. When they care for one another, they can care for animals, they can care for the land. When we are forced to live in large communities, this caring breaks down and we risk the survival of everything. We must go back to having an existence that has a human face, a place where human beings care (Keeney, 1994:124).

REFERENCES

Arbman, E. *Ecstasy or Religious Trance*, vol.1-3. Stockholm: Scandinavian University Books, 1963-1970.

Benz, E. *Dreams, Hallucinations and Visions.* New York: The Swedenborg Foundation, 1982.

Bohm, David. *Wholeness and the Implicate Order*. London: Ark Paperbacks, 1983.

Bootzin, R. R. "The role of expectancy in behavior change," *Placebo: Theory, Research, & Mechanisms.* New York: Guildford Press, 1985.

Bucke, Richard. *Cosmic Consciousness: A Study in the Evolution of the Human Mind.* New York: E. P. Dutton & Co., 1964, 22nd edition.

Campbell, Don, comp. *Music and Miracles*. Wheaton, IL: Quest Books, 1992.

_____. *Music, Physician for Times to Come*. Wheaton, IL: Quest Books, 1991.

Cayce, H. L. *Venture Inward*. New York: Harper & Row, 1964.

Cirlot, J. E. *A Dictionary of Symbols*, transl. J. Sage. New York: Philosophical Library, 1971. (originally published 1962).

Cousins, Norman. "Quotation," *Noetic Sciences Review*, 22 (Summer 1992): 3.

Cushing, Frank Hamilton. *Zuni Folk Tales*. Tucson, AZ: University of Arizona Press, 1986, pp. 150-174.

Csikszentmihalyi, M. "The flow experience and its significance for human psychology," *Optimal Experience: Psychological Studies of Flow in Consciousness*, eds M. and I. S. Csikszentmihalyi. Cambridge, MA: Cambridge University Press, 1988:15-35.

Dean, S. R. "Beyond the unconscious: the ultraconscious," A Journal of Psychiatry, 12:471 (1965).

de Boismont, A, and J.P. Brierre. A History of Dreams, Visions, Apparitions, Ecstacy, Magnnetism, and Somnabulism. Philadelphia, PA: Lindsay and Blakiston, 1855.

Deikman, Arthur J. "Deautomatization and the Mystic Experience," *Altered States of Consciousness*, ed. Charles T. Tart. New York: John Wiley & Sons, Inc., 1969, pp. 23-43.

Dourley, J. P. *The Psyche as Sacrament: A Comparative Study of C. G. Jung and Paul Tillich.* Toronto, Canada: Inner City Books, 1981.

Ehrenwald, Jan. *Psychotherapy: Myth and Method*. New York: Grune & Stratton. 1966.

Eisenbud, Jule. *Psi and Psychoanalysis*. New York: Grune & Stratton, 1970.

Emerson, Ralph Waldo. Essays: First Series Boston, MA: James Munroe and Company, 1884.

Eliade, Mircea. *The Sacred and the Profane: The Nature of Religion*, transl. W. R. Trask. New York: Harcourt, Brace & World, Inc., 1959.

Erdoes, Richard. *Crying for a Dream*. Santa Fe, NM: Bear & Company, 1990.

Erickson, Carolly. *The Medieval Vision* New York: Oxford University Press, 1976.

Feinstein, A. D. and Stanley Krippner. *Personal Mythology: The Psychology of Your Evolving Self.* Los Angeles, CA: J. P. Tarcher, 1988.

Foulkes, David, "Theories of Dream Formation and Recent Studies of Sleep Consciousness," *Altered States of Consciousness,* ed. Charles T. Tart, New York: John Wiley & Sons, Inc., 1969, pp. 117-131.

Foster, Steven. "Crying for a Vision, the Purpose Circle, and Emergence," *Proceedings of the Third International Conference on the Study of Shamanism and Alternate Modes of Healing,* August 30 to September 1, 1986, ed. Ruth-Inge Heinze. Madison, WI: A-R Editions, 1987, pp. 264-271.

Freud, Sigmund. *The Interpretation of Dreams.* London: Allen & Unwin, 1954.

Galton, Francis. "The Visions of Sane Persons," *Popular Science Monthly,* 19 (August. 1981):519-531.

Gaskell, G. A, *Dictionary of All Scriptures and Myths.* New York: Gramercy Books, 1981.

Goldberg, P. *The Intuitive Edge: Understanding Intuition and Applying it in Everyday Life.* Los Angeles, CA: J. P. Tarcher, Inc., 1983.

Goodman, Felicitas D. "The Lines of Nazca: A New Hypothesis," *Proceedings of the Tenth International Conference on the Study of Shamanism and Alternate Modes of Healing,* September 4-5, 1993, ed, Ruth-Inge Heinze. Berkeley, CA: Independent Scholars of Asia, Inc., 1993, pp. 262-269.

_____. "Visions," *The New Encyclopedia of Religion,* chief ed. Mircea Eliade, vol. 15. Chicago, IL: University of Chicago Press, 1987, pp. 287-288.

Govinda, Lama Anagarika. *The Way of the White Clouds.* Bombay, India: R. T. Publications, 1977.

Halifax, J., ed. *Shamanic Voices: A Survey of Visionary Narratives.* New York: E. P. Dutton, 1979.

Hardy, A. *The Spiritual Nature of Man.* Oxford, England: Clarendon Press, 1979.

Heinze, Ruth-Inge. "Visions of the 20th Century," *Proceedings of the International Conference on the Study of Shamanism and Alternate Modes of Healing,* ed. Ruth-Inge Heinze. Berkeley, CA: Independent Scholars of Asia, Inc., 1992a, pp. 1-9.

_____. "Inner Listening," *Music and Miracles,* comp. Don Campbell. Wheaton, IL: Quest Books, 1992b, pp. 128-136.

_____. *Shamans of the 20th Century.* New York: Irving Publishers, 1991.

_____. *Trance and Healing in Southeast Asia Today.* Bangkok/Berkeley: White Lotus/Independent Scholars of Asia, Inc., 1988

_____. "Don't let the Spirit Die," *Phoenix: The Journal of Transpersonal Anthropology:* VIII: 1-2 (1985):53-73.

Hilgard, J. R. *Personality and Hypnosis: A Study of Imaginative Involvement.* Chicago, IL: University of Chicago Press, 2nd ed., 1979.

Horowitz, M. J. *Image Formation and Cognition.* New York: Meredith Corp. 1970.

Houston, Jean. *The Search for the Beloved: Journeys in Sacred Psychology.* Los Angeles, CA: Jeremy P. Tarcher, Inc., 1987.

Hurston, Zora Neal. *The Sanctified Church*. Berkeley, CA: Turtle Island, 1983.

Huxley, A. *The Doors of Perception*. New York: Harper & Row, 1963.

Jamal, Michele. *Shape Shifters: Shaman Women in Contemporary Society*. New York and London: Arkana, 1987.

James, William. *The Varieties of Religious Experience*. New York: Mentor Books, 3rd ed., 1961. (first published in 1902)

John of the Cross. *Dark Night of the Soul*, transl. & ed. E. Allison Peers from the critical edition of P. Silverio de Santa Teresa, CD. G arden City, NY: Doubleday, Image Books, 1959.

Jung, C. G. Psychological Types, vol. 6., transl. R. F. C. Hull, eds H. Read, M. Fordham, G. Adler, & W. McGuire. Princeton: Princeton University Press, 2nd ed., 1971. (first published, with appendix, in 1960)

Kakar, Sudhir. *Shamans, Mystics, and Doctors: A Psychological Inquiry into India and its Healing Traditions*. Boston, MA: Beacon Press, 1982.

Keeney, Bradley. *Shaking Out the Spirits: A Psychotherapist's Entry into the Healing Mysteries of Global Shamanism*. Barrytown/ Station Hill Press, NY: 1994.

Krippner, Stanley and Joseph Dillard. *Dreamworking: How to Use Your Dreams For Creative Problem-Solving*. Buffalo, NY: Bearly Limited, 1988.

Kryder, Rowena Pattee. "Personal Crisis: Creativity and Culture-Making," *Creative Harmonics Institute Newsletter* (1993):1-2.

La Berge, Stephen. *Lucid Dreaming: The Power of Being Awake and Aware in Your Dreams*. Los Angeles, CA: Jeremy P. Tarcher, Inc., 1985.

Lame Deer, John (Fire) and Richard Erdoes. *Lame Deer, Seeker of Visions*. New York: Simon & Schuster, Inc., 1972.

Mails, Thomas E. *Fools Crow: Wisdom and Power*. Tulsa, OK: Council Oak Books, 1991.

Maslow, A. H. *The Farther Reaches of Human Nature*. New York: Penguin, 1983.

_____. *Religions, Values, and Peak Experiences*. New York: Penguin, 1964.

Masters, Robert and Jean Houston. *Mind Games*. New York: Dorset Press, 1972.

Maupin, Edward W. "On Meditation," *Altered States of Consciousness*, ed. Charles T. Tart. New York: John Wiley & Sons, Inc., 1969, pp. 177-186.

Metzner, Ralph. *Opening to Inner Light: The Transformation of* Human *Nature and Consciousness*. Los Angeles: Jeremy P. Tarcher, Inc., 1986.

Mooney, James. *The Ghost Dance Religion and Wounded Knee*. New York: Dover, 1973.

Murphy, Michael. *The Future of the Body: Explorations into the Further Evolution of Human Nature*. Los Angeles, CA: Jeremy P. Tarcher, Inc., 1992.

_____. "The Future of the Body, a Conversation with Michael Murphy," interviewer Ronald S. Miller, *Noetic Sciences Review*, 22 (Summer 1992):6-14.

Neher, Andrew. *The Psychology of Transcendence*. New York: Dover Publications, Inc., 1990.

Neihardt, John G. *Black Elk Speaks: Being the Life Story of a Holy Man of the Oglala Sioux*. Lincoln, NB: University of Nebraska Press, 1961.

Nietzsche, F. *The Genealogy of Morals: An Attack*, transl. F. Golfing. Garden City, NY: Doubleday Anchor, 1956. (first published 1887)

Noll, R. "Mental imagery cultivation as a cultural phenomenon: The role of visions in shamanism," *Current Anthropology*, 26: 5(1985):1-60.

Nyanaponika Thera. *The Heart of Buddhist Meditation: A Handbook of Mental Training Based on the Buddha's Way of Mindfulness*. New York: The Citadel Press, 1969.

Otto, Rudolf. *Mysticism East and West: A Comparative Analysis of the Nature of Mysticism*, transls Bertha L. Bracey and Richenda C. Payne. New York: Living Age Books, 1957.

Pike, Nelson. *Mystic Union: An Essay in the Phenomenology of Mysticism*. Ithaca, NY: Cornell University Press, 1992.

Pinkson, Thomas. *A Quest For Vision*. San Francisco: Saybrook Institute, Ph.D. dissertation, 1976.

Prabhavananda, Swami and Christopher Isherwood. *How to Know God: The Yoga Aphorism of Patanjali*. New York: The New American Library, 1953.

Progoff, Ira. *The Practice of Process Meditation: The Intensive Journal Way to Spiritual Experience*. New York: Dialogue House Library, 1980.

Puree, Jill. *The Mystic Spiral: Journey of the Soul*. London: Thames & Hudson, 1974.

Remen, Rachel Naomi. "Quotation," *Noetic Science Review*, 28 (Winter 1993):41.

Rilke, Rainer Maria. "Quotation," *Noetic Science Review*, 22 (Summer 1992):48.

Roszak, Theodore. "The Voice of the Earth," *Noetic Sciences Review*, 22 (Summer 1992):15-18.

Schwarz, Berthold. *Psychic-Dynamics*. New York: Pageant Press, 1965.

Stace, Walter T. *The Teaching of the Mystics*. New York: New American Library, 1960.

Stafford, William. "A Ritual We Read to Each Other," *Noetic Sciences Review*, 28 (Winter 1993):15.

St. Ignatius of Loyola. The Spiritual Exercises of St. Ignatius, transl. Anthony Mottola. New York: Doubleday, 1964.

St. John of the Cross. *The Dark Night of the Soul*, transl. E. Allison Peers. Garden City, NY: Doubleday & Co., 1959.

Tart, Charles T. ed. *Altered States of Consciousness*. New York: John Wiley & Sons, Inc., 1969.

_____. *Waking Up: Overcoming the Obstacles of Human Potential*. Boston, MA: Shambhala, New Sciences Library, 1986.

Taylor, Eugene. "Our Roots: The American Visionary Tradition," *Noetic Science Review*, 27 (Autumn 1993):6-17.

Ullman, M. "Dreaming, Life-style, and Physiology: A Comment on Adler's View of the Dream," *Journal of Individual Psychology*, 18 (1962):18-25.

_____ and M. Zimmerman. *Working With Dreams*. Los Angeles, CA: Jeremy P. Tarcher, Inc., 1979.

Underhill, Evelyn. *Mysticism: A Study in the Nature and Development of Man's Spiritual Consciousness*. New York: Noonday Press, 1955.

Ven. U. Silananda. *The Four Foundations of Mindfulness*, ed. Ruth-Inge Heinze. Boston, MA: Wisdom Publications, 1990.

White, J., ed. *The Highest State of Consciousness*. Garden City, NY: Anchor Books, 1972.

Wittgenstein, L. *Philosophical Investigations*, transl. G. E. M. Anscombe. Oxford, UK: Basil Blackwell, 1953.

Young, Arthur. The *Reflexive Universe: Evolution of Consciousness*. Mill Valley, CA: Robert Briggs Association, 1976.

INDEX

www.ingramcontent.com/pod-product-compliance
Lightning Source LLC
Chambersburg PA
CBHW062208270326
41930CB00009B/1681